CHICAGO QUARTERLY REVIEW™

Volume 20
The Italian Issue
Spring 2015

Cover illustration "Il leone della piccola Pauline" by Rossana Campo, from *L'arte soppianta tutti gli altri enzimi. Opere 2000-2011*, Il Canneto Editore, 2012.

The Chicago Quarterly Review is published by The Chicago Quarterly Review 501(c)3 in Evanston, Illinois. Unsolicited submissions are welcome through our submissions manager at Submittable. To find out more about us, please visit www.chicagoquarterlyreview.com.

TABLE OF CONTENTS

EDITOR'S NOTE

In this special issue, the *Chicago Quarterly Review* turns its attention to Italy and its writers during a time of great unrest, both socially and politically. We searched long and hard for over a year and unearthed quite a few literary gems. Emerging Italian writers came to us with their writings eager to promote them in another language and bring their words to America. English-speaking writers, translators, and academicians proposed work in translation of more established Italian authors active from the 1960s on. All these pieces eventually came together ready to dialogue with each other and with our readers, thanks to the patient, bridge-building art of translation.

The result is a diverse, vibrant collection of poetry and prose that spans from the second half of the 20th century to nowadays, encompasses different topics, and includes a wide variety of different styles and colors, from avant-garde to commercial writing and all that is in between. We found a strong sample of women writers who are representative of Italy's changing literary scene. Since the mid-20th century, the rise of women authors in Italy has brought to light new points of view and sensibilities. We appreciated the emergence of urgent contemporary topics in several of the writings that were submitted: the fall of ideologies, homosexuality, transgenderism, new technologies, cancer. We enjoyed seeing the manifold dance of poetry through the decades, always suspended between classic inspirations and the desire to break free from them. We rediscovered the past with the only non-fiction piece of this collection that brings us back to a recent time when Italy was the theater of World War II, and people of good will and extreme courage fought to save their lives, the lives of others, and the immense gift of art.

We organized these pieces in a loosely chronological order so that our American readers will have a better sense of how to situate them historically. We've mixed poetry and fiction because we do not believe in a strong separation between the two literary genres; we like the idea of one spilling into the other and inspiring readers to push the boundaries of their comfort zones and explore something new. Finally we made sure that this would be an enjoyable experience, full of sparkling surprises first page to last. *Buona lettura!*

Michela Martini, Guest Editor

Juan Rodolfo Wilcock was born in Buenos Aires in 1919 and studied civil engineering there, but quickly turned his attentions to literature, becoming part of the Borges circle in the 1940s. He left Argentina in 1951, briefly residing in London but eventually settling in Rome. From then on he wrote his fiction, poetry, essays, and journalism almost exclusively in Italian. He is best known for his 1972 novel, *La sinagoga degli iconoclasti* (*The Temple of Iconoclasts*). Wilcock died in Lubriano, Italy, in 1978. His *Poesie* was published by Adelphi in 1980.

The following poems belong to the section "Per il gatto," which is part of *Luoghi comuni*, originally published by Il Saggiatore in 1961.

THE EXILE

J. Rodolfo Wilcock

A sunbeam on the water,
only one word on the lip
here at the spring's well where
a stone bee seems to sip.

Find that word alone,
become again for a moment
in this exile that is torment
the poet you are no more.

Translated by Bonnie Costello

INNOCENT DREAM

J. Rodolfo Wilcock

I don’t want to be what I am anymore.
I want to be a monstrous bug
with giant black feelers.
And everyone would worship me.

In my lovers I’d inspire
fear and submission,
and I’d pay their long services
with a shower of gold.

Each evening I’d massacre
moralists and orators,
then break in from windows
and splay myself over naked girls,

while the crowd from the street
applauds and obeys,
eating the meat of the dead,
drinking the blood of the rich.

And I’m not far off,
And I’m not far off,
this dream might come true.

Translated by Bonnie Costello

TO DISMANTLE MYSELF

J. Rodolfo Wilcock

I reach across my past
vain tentacles of dream
to pry out objects, papers,
that may not be there now;
yet, I've a qualm, I know
my symbolic riches remain,
in that house closed up today,
cage of a madman and a crone:
portraits of me then,
the stencil with my name,
and above all me, me
in the mirrors, on the walls.
Come on, I should dismantle
this temple of myself,
ransack it, donate
to the museums my finest furnishings
and knock down the rest,
exorcise that place,
once a site for the cult of myself,
die without leaving
traces, good or bad,
get rid of it all, leave
the way I came.

Translated by Bonnie Costello

SPACE

J. Rodolfo Wilcock

In my room there is nothing
but the phonograph and a bed;
likewise in the heart, there is nothing
of me, but a stranger instead.

So there is space to move about
whether in the heart or in the room;
I have thrown the tatters in the hearth,
the feelings I've thrown into the sea.

Not everyone has an empty room,
not everyone has an empty heart:
here one can let in
a new world every morning.

Translated by Bonnie Costello

THE FIRST ONES

J. Rodolfo Wilcock

They were wandering in the garden, and he perceived
in the surrounding phosphorescent glimmer
the agitation of the first lover;
they were wandering in silence, Adam and Eve,

and an azure haze was enveloping
from the azure foliage and the panting
humid night of summer heat so stifling
a lamp on the horizon was relighting.

They were just born, but some unconscious will
was driving the dark ones toward the ocean
extending to the feet of that dark hill.

And they embraced, and into the labyrinth
they entered, that can never be undone,
the maze of the impure, of repetition.

Translated by Bonnie Costello

THE NIGHT OF SAN GIOVANNI

J. Rodolfo Wilcock

Slowly like an animal
that circles and is meek,
tied to a center pole,
today the sun reaches the peak
of the boreal eclipse,
and on tracks already traced
in its diurnal rounds
now tips the urn down,
making a summer flurry
on the Euphrates and the Missouri.

Today all the Northern region
at the door of the season
makes solstice celebration;
the female forms a passion
for conjugal duty,
conceiving in the blaze
of fires and illuminations
the new generations
that on love's pretext meet
to deliver the heat.

This is the fecund time;
meanwhile those abiding
at the world's other extreme
prepare themselves for the rigors
of the meditative cold
that falls from mute mountains
in wave upon wave
as a frozen foam scatters
the waste around
on gray emaciated ground.

Translated by Bonnie Costello

Guido Morselli was born in Bologna in 1912. In the 1930s, he earned a law degree and served in the Italian army; called up again in 1940 when Italy entered the war, he wrote a study of his beloved Marcel Proust. In 1943, Italy surrendered and Morselli waited out the war in Calabria. Afterwards this lonely, gifted, eccentric writer settled in provincial Lombardy, where he lived very frugally and in relative solitude.

Morselli was a literary outsider who conformed to no late modernist school. His novels—*Roma senza papa, Contropassato-prossimo* (translated in English as *Past-Conditional*), *Divertimento* 1889 (same title in English), and *Dissipatio H.G.*—are maniacally documented, counterfactual, subtly apocalyptic. *The Communist* (original title: *Il comunista*, 1964), about a melancholy functionary of the Italian Communist Party in the Khrushchev years, has more in common with the novels of Andrei Platonov than with any of the Soviet dissidents of the period. Morselli's non-partisan human sympathy for party hack Walter Ferranini was unusual during the Cold War and heightened his uncanny prophecy about the collapse of the Soviet dream. Unable to find a publisher for any of his novels, Morselli shot himself in 1973. The following year, Adelphi began releasing his works to considerable critical acclaim.

The following is an excerpt from *Il comunista*, Adelphi, 1976.

THE COMMUNIST

Guido Morselli

Debate (repose) in Parliament. It was question time and the conditions, dreadful, of the State Railways were the subject at hand. The Chamber's population, already sparse, had shrunk further as always happened when technical matters were being discussed—all but the left-wing benches, where the questioner sat. Despite the back and forth between questioner and minister (Angelini) the atmosphere was drowsy; and a weak polemical note introduced by the far right brought only a flicker of mirth and annoyance. The interruption came from the neo-Fascist benches; the voice, with its stout Sicilian cadences, strove for irony.

"You complain that the trains arrive late. You understand, Honorable Boatta, do you not, that your criticism necessarily takes us back to those days when there was one man above all who could make the trains in Italy run on time?"

"And it cost us dearly," was Comrade Boatta's swift reply. But the other man persisted:

"Not only the trains ran, in those days. Sad to say, this lily-livered *Italia* of ours . . ."

Here Boatta lost his patience.

"Learn to speak Italian, Fascist! In Italian, we do not say *Itahl-yah.*"

"Right, I should learn from you. You, who say *Itaglia*, with the *g*. Peasant."

There was a titter from the center benches. Dini, deputy from Lucca, growled, "Oh, come on, you think we haven't noticed you don't even know how to say Italy?"

From his high seat as president of the Chamber, Leone leaned forward to make his presence felt and (a stab at wit) said that "from regionalisms" it was time to move on to "rails." Comrade Boatta raised his clipped grey beard once again and observed that there was nothing in the least bourgeois about wanting trains that respected timetables, rail cars that were modern, conductors dressed in decent cloth and not some shabby worsted.

"It is not only the bourgeoisie who use trains but above all the workers, just as it is workers who make them run. With toil and sacrifices, as Ferranini, here next to me, can tell you, being the son of a railman who died on the job, and a railman himself."

"Furthermore," the elderly Boatta plowed on, to the revived indifference of his colleagues, "beyond the railroads we have other public services that are backward and badly organized. Is the telephone system, so important for production and by extension for the workers, at all satisfactory? The Italian postal service is the slowest in Europe. This morning I received a letter here in Rome. My niece mailed it two days ago in Turin."

Now Leone intervened.

"You asked to question the Transport Minister," he croaked, "not the Minister of Posts. And spare us your personal correspondence, it is of no interest!"

Comrade Ferranini, who was just barely listening, smiled, feeling pleasantly lethargic. Sitting at his bench, his elbows pointing down at the desktop, he ran his hands though his greying hair. He was taking his repose, and he didn't even need to reproach himself: how very pleasant. When Comrade Boatta had said his name, he had for one incongruous moment been afraid he would be called on to speak; he, who in five months of parliamentary session had never even spoken once. He had been assigned to a committee that met rarely, the most pacific and least industrious committee there was, in which his silence was no more remarked upon than it was in the Chamber. The party, too, asked little of him, perhaps because in Rome, where he had never set foot in the party headquarters before his recent election, nobody knew him. Apart from a few inspections on behalf of the administrative offices, he had no duties at all. On Sundays, there were the rallies assigned to members of Parliament in turn; so far, he had held no more than three or four.

Ferranini, Walter. From Reggio Emilia. The last to know that "Italy's Kiev[1]" was well-represented by him. Both the shortcomings and the merits.

A real man of the base, accustomed to the base's lively, immediate, human political contact. By no means free of any personal ambitions, but Ferranini had always confined them to his local environment and satisfied them there. When he had agreed to stand for Parliament it had cost him some considerable remorse, a fear of betraying his real calling, an unease from which he was just beginning to recover. To his comrades in Reggio who had put him on the list, he said, "So, you are sending me into retirement." And in some ways, he did feel he had been set aside. He could not pretend, in those intervals he spent back home, to recover that connection between himself and his people that had been interrupted, nor could he resume his previous responsibilities. In Rome (and this he had predicted) no opportunities presented themselves in the party hierarchy, and quite honestly, he recognized he was neither prepared, nor keen for any such role. The twelve years of work behind him were not relevant, and his experience organizing was too specialized to employ in a much larger sphere, far from the situations and the men familiar to him.

In other ways, he hadn't been unhappy in Rome, and he had ended up settling there. When he returned to Reggio or to his native Vimondino, some twenty kilometers from Reggio, he stayed one day at most. He didn't mind the parliamentary routine, the way that deputies in a great party clung together ("Here, we are choristers with our mouths shut," he wrote to the faithful Oscar Fubini). There were no decisions to take, no initiatives; however, he told Fubini, there was much to learn and much to understand. He had come to terms with parliamentarianism. He no longer thought of how, during the electoral campaign of '53 in the days of the *legge-truffa*[2], the fraudulent new voting law, he had called Parliament (employing a certain scientific slant that ran through his speeches) the "locus of points" of phony formal democracy. Study had always been a passion of his, and he had nearly always had too little time for it. Now, with many free hours

Translator's Notes:

1. The Emilia region, then largely devoted to agriculture, was one of Italy's reddest.
2. The so-called "con act" introduced by the Christian Democrats and fiercely opposed by the Communists gave sixty-five percent of the seats in Parliament to the coalition holding fifty percent plus one vote.

a day, he was able to satisfy that desire. His knowledge of Marxism, although it was first-hand, was disorganized, incoherent. He applied himself to perfecting it, tenaciously, scrupulously; it seemed to him a way to resist inertia and conformity; it was what a good socialist would do. Those few who tried to flush him out at his lodgings on Via del Leonetto, lodgings that were not very inviting, and he even less so, found him taking notes on the classics, intense and ruffled, in shirt sleeves, like a student preparing for his exams. A thermos full of coffee and—that final touch that completed the modest genre painting—a bird cage on the windowsill. He was growing lazy; it annoyed him to have to drag himself out to Civitavecchia or Rieti for the Saturday or Sunday rally, he, who back in Reggio would travel the length and breadth of the province all week, running automobiles into the ground and coming back at night hoarse and exhausted.

Conscientious about his inertia, and perhaps the only one there who didn't attribute his idleness to scirocco or Roman habits, he wondered if it wasn't a symptom of premature aging. Or worse, far worse, the first sign of petit-bourgeois regression. One night he rose from his bed and paged uneasily through his texts to see whether sloth was not one of the symptoms by which one could recognize those whom Marx called "vacillators." Luck was with him, and he found the passage right away ("The vacillators are the weak, half-hearted, and irresolute") and went back to sleep peacefully.

It was his enduring good fortune that he paid only moderate attention to his own, private ego. Soul searching and inner dialogues were neither lengthy nor frequent with him; it was just that after forty-four good years, the fatigue had become too much. He had played out his role. Started out as a kid slaving and toiling away; never enjoyed even a bit of the good life; well, now he felt the need to take it easy for a while. A man to dispose of, no; now that he'd been in Rome for a while things were improving, although a few little troubles remained: that ache at the base of his neck, some signs of hypertension, some shortness of breath, a bit of arrhythmia, which one of his parliamentary colleagues, comrade Amoruso, an internist, had diagnosed (informally, without having examined him because Ferranini preferred not) as chronic fatigue accompanied by mild, functional heart disease, in part psychogenic. The party, by bringing him to Rome to rest, had showed him its providential participation in the life of the individual; he would employ that to fully restore his health. A new call to action might come at any moment, and in the meantime, to sit there in the Chamber with his comrades and his superiors was not to do nothing. Even there, one served. There was certainly nothing wrong with that. If anything, he thought (but not sanctimoniously, that wasn't his way) it was a privilege he didn't deserve.

Boatta had finished. He stated that Angelini's reply was unsatisfactory, and in fact it was not very satisfactory, and then other questions were raised, now by the Christian Democratic side, in collusion with the government. Sham, of no interest. Ferranini sat back more comfortably in his seat and gave up looking through the newspapers he'd brought with him. Two rows below him, Olinto Maccagni[3] was going through his mail, writing undisturbed; there was a little pile of books on his desktop, and Ferranini was able to make out the title of the one on top. Montaigne, *Essais*. For a long time, he gazed respectfully at what he could see of the person of his leader. The thick, still-dark hair on his head; the motionless, firm shoulders and forearms, which bespoke a serenity and a force that seemed to him majestic, uniting ideas and action. Then he gave a start: Maccagni had stopped writing, turned halfway around, and was staring at him through thick lenses. But he didn't recognize him. He was famous for not recognizing faces, and they had only had the briefest of contacts. No matter: Ferranini savored the composite pleasure of trust and subordination; he felt happy he somehow belonged to this man.

Among the newspapers on his desktop he picked out a telegram that had been delivered to him at the beginning of the session. It came from Reggio, from home, in short, the only (large!) family he had. It informed him that two friends were coming to Rome, leaders of the Farmers' Cooperative of Guastella, and he had to smile because the two had signed themselves "Amos and Vittorio Bignami, directing Italy's first kolkhoz." What did you want to bet they had already arrived and were there in the Chamber? He looked up, and there they were, in fact, the very same. The sole spectators to that colorless assembly, fists up to salute him, two scrappy cousins with red carnations in their buttonholes sitting in the public gallery. He signaled back at them to remain calm; they were capable of shouting out loud and making themselves obvious, and Maccagni wouldn't have liked that. He waited, leafing through the newspapers, until the other man moved. Maccagni continued writing, sitting at his place for another half hour, until eight o'clock, and meanwhile those two up there could be seen talking back and forth and pointing out the various party benches in the Chamber.

Outside, they embraced, and not long after, examining him by the light of a shop window on the street, Amos Bignami reassured him. "You haven't changed." Ferranini misunderstood.

---

3. The name suggests that of Palmiro Togliatti, general secretary of the Italian Communist Party (PCI) from 1927-1964.

"Should I have changed? You mean Parliament, maybe? Or Rome?"

"No, no, don't be silly. You're still thin, sure; still have that look of a kid, or a poet. Our Ferranini, you are. Hey, we came here for you, you know, to tell you about Vimondino, that little town of yours half-flooded by the River Po."

"Always under water in November, that home town of ours. Why don't you ever come to ask for help against the Farm Owners Consortium instead?"

"Well, so you know we're fighting them, like mad. *Como los moros*. Kruger against Lopez, remember in Spain? Like that! We don't have a choice, believe me. They're going after us. There have been some changes in the Federation, but you know about that."

"And how are things going with Inter-Agraria?"

"Not so smooth there either. We'll tell you about it."

He led the way to his trattoria on a side street near via dei Coronari, a place not haunted by his parliamentary colleagues, and therefore to his liking. The two Bignamis, Amos more than Vittorio, reported at length, in that polite and deferential way of resourceful subordinates (Ferranini had never done much more than outline the political directives with them) and then went on to recount the news in town. They didn't live there, but each of them had a piece of land nearby, and they knew everyone, and everything. They spoke at length, not eating much. Ferranini ate happily, as usual. Bent over his plate, his left hand pressing a napkin to his chest, with great concentration, although he listened and asked a question now and then. A frugal man, with a liking for simple things, that is; but one who enjoyed his food, in silence if possible; it seemed (and it wasn't just semblance) that when he ate, he thought of nothing else. His lady friend, Nuccia (or better, Annuccia), had decided that though there was no hint of sensuality to it, he was a "serious eater," that is to say, profound, even in that, and scrupulous; while he pointed out to her that he came from a family that had suffered from pellagra—from hunger in other words—right up into the twentieth century.

Vittorio Bignami, abstemious although he had the purple cheeks of a wine drinker, had been Ferranini's first aide back in '46 when he began working in the cooperatives, and he wanted to know whether he was still dealing with the co-ops here in Rome, and if they'd given him duties in that regard, and what they were. He was astonished to hear they hadn't.

"Okay, but really, Ferranini, you have nothing to do with them? You, one of the greatest cooperativists of our times?"

"Sure. And the Farmers' Co-op of Guastella is a kolkhoz," said Ferranini. He had finished eating and now resumed speaking.

"They don't appreciate you? What about il Migliore[4], doesn't he know you? You were sitting close by one another."

"There are one hundred and forty of us in the lower house alone. But look, you ought to know that the base is one thing, the center is another: two worlds, like water and air, you might say, and the man who lives in one isn't made to live in the other; he doesn't have the organs."

"It's not right."

"It's perfectly right. I'm here to represent the base, not to advance it from above. Different functions, different capacities. I go to party headquarters a couple of times a month, and I still haven't learned how the departments are divided up. You have to understand that the party here is a huge, complex structure. But let's talk about what we know, my friends. Vimondino. Honest territory, rich territory, but a bit dull, eh?"

"Oh come on, *Ferranin*! Dull. Dull!"

It was a territory of land-owning farmers and not even such very small farmers; many of them had twenty, twenty-five *biolche* or more. (One biolca: about 3,000 square meters). The town coasted the railway that ran down from Reggio to the Po River; around there they called it the land of priests and poplars, something of an exaggeration when it came to priests, of which there were only two, the parish priest and the chaplain of San Donato, but certainly it was a politically thankless place. Scarce in support for the progressive parties, more open to the Christian Democratic side, not without a deeply-rooted residue of Fascism, with 290 votes (out of 1,200) for the neo-fascist party in the '53 election. Land ownership in Vimondino had begun in the twentieth century. That is, with the demise of the feudal lord, a certain Count Giarrentani for whom the Vimondinesi had worked as sharecroppers.

Around 1902, his appetite whetted by the fortune one of his former tenants had made in Modena manufacturing cured meats, Giarrentani opened his own cured meats company in Reggio and began to pursue a brisk competition with the other man, even imitating his brand name. The first contemplated revenge. He waited until the bully count had expanded and put all his capital into the company, then in a few short months, lowering his prices week by week, he drove him to the point where he had to sacrifice his factory and then his lands. Giarrentani was barely able to hold onto the villa where he lived in Vimondino, and he had to endure the humiliation of seeing his old sharecroppers become his peers, for the winner of the match, who had no interest in keeping

4. "The Best," as Togliatti was known.

the lands, sold them one after the other at very convenient prices, and so for once, a war between capitalists brought forth good fortune to the workers.

The town was the only one in the province of Reggio to produce hemp, a hemp famous for its quality; the buyers arrived from England and snapped it all up. Under King George, the ropes on more than one of His Majesty's ships were woven with Vimondinese hemp. The sharecroppers-become-bosses recruited field hands (going up in the Apennines to find them) for the hardest work. And they basked in their indolence, their miserly well-being, quite extraneous to the political energy of the rest of the province, and indeed to Emilia *tout court.* The impatient socialist Ferranini once held a rally in Vimondino; no one showed up, and he refused to go back there. The town produced a couple of interventionists between March and May 1915[5] and later quite a few *squadristi* ready to take part in the tamer exploits of the Bolognese Fascist boss Leandro Arpinati.

Amos, the older of the two Bignami cousins and older than Ferranini himself, could remember a thing or two from those earlier days.

"Arpinati treated the people from Vimondino like chicken thieves. His exact words were: "You people are only good for swiping chickens."

Among the few, none of them born there, the one who kept his eyes open politically was Mirko Ferranini, Walter's father, who had come from Cesena to Reggio in '10 to work as a fireman on the Reggio-Guastella line. As a young man he'd belonged to a cell of anarchists, an offshoot of that Bakunin League of Young Romagna that had given the movement some of its least hot-headed and most coherent men, such as Capriani. But even Mirko, who had married in '16 after he was promoted to engineer, grew tame. A railway engineer is a precision instrument, he would say, and it was clear that meant a man of order. The red leagues after the war, the popular uprisings in Emilia against the growing forces of reaction, had little effect on Vimondino, or on Mirko Ferranini either. Only in the spring of '21, when in America, in Dedham, Massachusetts, Sacco and Vanzetti were incriminated and threatened with the electric chair (not a vain threat, as it turned out) did Mirko begin to come back to life. They were martyrs of his old faith, and suffering with them, although far away, he finally felt himself redeemed. He wrote to the elder of the two, Bartolomeo Vanzetti, and some months later he had a reply from prison. He wrote again, and Vanzetti replied, and in the last of those letters he said, "Yes, all power to anarchism, but now we must close ranks. It would be wrong to spend our forces and squander

5. The months before Italy entered WWI.

our hopes. The revolution that has triumphed over the Tsar is a worthy cause for the sons of Bakunin." The engineer, who had decorated the kitchen and bedroom of his house with photographs of the martyrs cut from the newspapers, did not understand poor Vanzetti's counsel, or decided not to speak about it, but the seed bore fruit in his son. Walter Ferranini (one of the few Italian Communists of today to have read the works of Malatesta[6] and other masters of anarchism) was a socialist even before he became a man.

He got there all by himself, without knowing (without any way of knowing, in Italy between '29 and '34) that socialist doctrine existed, or socialist reality. He glimpsed certain truths—the pure formality of liberty; the capitalist depersonalization of the individual and of human life—on his own, in a sudden burst of revelation, the way a fifteen year old boy will guess what a woman's body is like. But he was, and would remain, a simple soul, despite a rude speculative instinct that pushed him to seek out ideas, to dig into them; and he was modest, although spontaneous and direct, qualities that usually didn't accompany modesty. He never made much of his political education, although it was certainly precocious. More than once Ferranini had thought, and said, perhaps even to one of the Bignami cousins, "If I am a good socialist, I cannot take the credit. I couldn't lean toward the right side because that was to go against nature. Nor toward the left in the sense of anarcho-syndicalist, because that made me think of Vanzetti; I'd been immunized for life against that side." (He had kept those three letters and promised himself he would go and pay homage to the tombs of Sacco and Vanzetti, wherever they might be.)

He too suffered from temptations. But not of the faith; if anything, it was his vocation as a militant that was threatened. His greatest temptation was tied to a peculiar, vital craving, of mysterious origin but already quite overwhelming when he was just a child growing up in the country, a child who in summertime would lie on his stomach looking down into the pits where the hemp was retted (they gave off a stink worse than the sewer), brooding on the fauna of worms and larvae that swarmed on the greenish slime of the water's surface. That same craving sent him into town to search the market stalls for tattered old editions of Fabre's *Insects*, or Maeterlinck's *Life of Termites*. A craving to flush the spiders out of the attic and the toads from the ditches, and classify them. A magnifying glass he'd been presented by the Zanasi, the teacher in Vimondino (from Ferrara and a Fascist, the same Zanasi who at Porta Po in Ferrara in '27 foiled the attempt on *ras* Italo Balbo's life), that poor magnifying glass was to hang from his neck for years on

6. Italian anarchist Enrico Malatesta (1853-1932).

a piece of twine.

Finally the craving became conscious, and thirteen-year-old Walter understood that to satisfy it would mean sacrifice, and what was harder, asking others to sacrifice. "All I can do," his father said to him, "is to let you keep on studying without considering you crazy or an ingrate." The boy was persistent, and lucky, too, for a while; he knocked on many doors and in Reggio found a pharmacist Bignami (another one) who had many children and took him in as a baby minder and shop boy and in return gave him room and board and allowed him to continue his education. He grew fond of him, and looked after him, and even got it in his head the boy might study to be a pharmacist. Ferranini turned to Amos who was taking his coffee.

"Oh, remember the pharmacist near the hospital? A widower, with a lot of children?"

"I certainly do; he was a relative of ours," said Amos. "Distant relative. One of those pale-faced socialists, á la Turati[7]. You know what happened to him right after the Great War, in Bologna?"

"No."

"You, Vittorio, did you ever hear about it? The thing was that the Socialist Congress was being held in the Teatro Brunetti in Bologna, and Bignami the pharmacist, who was the organizer, met Anna Kuliscioff[8] and fell in love with her. And she with him, at the time. And you know, she was over fifty years old! All hell broke loose. Turati was as jealous as a wild animal; it almost led to another split among the socialists."

With the pharmacist's help, young Ferranini had finished the gymnasium and was doing his first year of *liceo*. His goal was approaching, it was becoming clearer before his enchanted eyes: Bologna, university, biology. "Biology," said Ferranini; it was a word that had once set him shivering like the name of a first love, just the sound of it. Then came that terrible December of '29. In just one month his father was dead of pneumonia and Walter had said farewell to school and was back in Guastella working as a loader at the rail depot to help out his mother. She'd been left with a ninety-lire pension, her mind was undone by misfortune, and the neighbors feared might throw herself under a train. It wasn't her head that failed though, but her heart; she died in '31, not even forty years old, of an aneurysm. That same year the Carabinieri found a packet of leaflets in the station depot where

---

7. Filippo Turati (1857-1932), respected leader of Italy's Socialist Party, founded in 1892 and split in 1921 when the Communist Party broke off. The latter considered Turati's reformers less than red-blooded.
8. (1857-1925) Russian born, Turati's partner; one of the leaders of the Italian Socialist Party.

the young man was working, leaflets he was supposed to take home with him that evening. To distribute among his apathetic, or hostile, fellow townsmen.

"Emilia has been, and shall be, Red," read the title at the top of the leaflet. Fired on the spot, an orphan without relatives or a home, young Walter had learned—directly, painfully—what the real world of work was like. At the depot he sometimes had to load, all by himself in one day, six thousand kilos of milk. Fatigue had marked him permanently and had clarified certain aspects and problems of labor that no theoretical study can ever teach. They took him on at a small shoe factory at San Donato (he stayed for seven years), and there too it was all toil: packer, driver, porter, loader, and unloader of crates, heavy rolls of leather, great demijohns of acid, from six in the morning to seven at night. He didn't have the constitution for heavy labor, and the weariness wasn't only impressed on the ideas in his head. When he was called up and went for his medical exam, they found a heart murmur.

* * *

That was a nice piece of luck, wasn't it; it meant they would give him an exemption. (He had finished eating and was going over that chapter of his life with the two cousins, letting the hour pass until it was time to get up from the table.) Because if the army hadn't rejected him, Abyssinia was waiting for him, and perhaps Spain[9].

"Instead," said Vittorio Bignami, "we went to Spain on the right side." He plowed on, certain of what he was saying:

"Which is why, you see, it makes no sense that you shouldn't get ahead here in Rome too. In the party. You've played all your cards right."

Ferranini, however, was annoyed by his insistence.

"First of all, remember that I wasn't here during the Resistance. Someone of our age who wasn't a partisan is a grade B communist."

"You weren't a partisan because you were in America. How long was it?"

"Five years."

"And it wasn't your fault. You went there after fighting in Spain because you couldn't come back here. And you've also been to the USSR. There aren't many like you."

---

9. In 1935–36 Italy fought a brutal war in Ethiopia before annexing the territory to its East Africa Colony. Some fifty thousand Italian "volunteers" were sent by Mussolini to fight with Franco in the Spanish Civil War. Other Italians went of their own accord to back the Republicans.

"Come on, friends, let's be serious," said Ferranini, not very nicely, his temper souring. "I spent forty days in the Ukraine, just about all of it in the countryside. What I know of the USSR is just about enough to be able to say that our cooperatives in Reggio Emilia . . ."

"*Your* cooperatives."

"Let's put it this way: there's night and day between them and a real collective enterprise. I mean in terms of mentality. I've said it over and over: what we do here gets done for our own filthy interests."

The Bignami cousins looked at each other and tried to laugh.

"My friends, there's little to laugh about. We are individualists, the opposite of socialists; we think about the land the way we think about a girl's titties. We lust for ownership, although we use the language of collectivism."

He grew heated as he expounded his argument. His seriousness was all out of proportion, which wasn't unusual in Ferranini.

"In Russia they may be less advanced than we are in terms of technology, say, machinery and seed, fertilizers, insecticides, silos, and dairies, baling, but let me say this, they have gone beyond that mentality of ours, that concupiscence. That is the difference, and get it into your heads, otherwise all my preaching is for nothing."

"It's the environment," said Vittorio, "the capitalist system."

"What the hell, boys, are we supposed to change the system or not?"

"We've had our coffee," said Amos, gently trying to distract him, "and we forgot the cheese course. What kind of Reggio natives are we?"

The waiter came to clear the table, and they asked him to bring cheese. Once again they ate in silence, although Vittorio did take the opportunity to admire the "titties" of two flowery, out of season female tourists (Germans, English? You had to be in Rome to see them) who were just then sitting down not far from their table. Amos was commenting on the cheese, a Reggiano, with his mouth full:

"This is our genuine stuff, made in winter, from two milkings. Once upon a time there was hardly any of it on the market; it didn't get as far as, I won't even say Rome, as far as Bologna. After the war, it was the steel vats instead of the wooden buckets, the electric heaters in the dairies, that made production expand, and for that to happen, as you know, Ferranini, we had to have workers' collectives like the farmers' cooperatives and the other cooperatives, we needed Collina, Maccaferri and (say it proud!) the Bignami cousins. We've done a lot, even if you're not content. There are billions that don't go in the bosses' pockets, that are divided by the workers."

Ferranini, still eating, shrugged his shoulders.

"You," Amos went on, "have always been too modest, in Spain, at home, here, everywhere. Did you tell them, at the party, that you can speak Russian? Did you tell them you correspond with the top scientists of the Soviet Union?"

Ferranini glanced around the room.

"Get out of here, Bignami. Hush. Soviet scientists have better things to do than write to me."

"Oh, we learned about it from Fubini in the Federation, isn't that right, Vittorio? What was he called, that big shot professor at the University of Moscow who wrote to you? Bosciàn?"

His face clouded once again.

"Stop this nonsense. It was I who wrote to him; I learned some Russian so that I could. I wrote to Oparin[10], to Bosciàn, to Lepescinskaia, back in '47 when I was still a kid in some ways. I had a passion for biology, and I used to study on my own. Oparin had just discovered the *Koatszervatnyi* mechanism, coacervates, it's a bit difficult to explain."

"Hey, Fubini told us they wrote to you too."

"Fubini should mind his own business. They replied to me, and that was it. I remember that Bosciàn, one of the greatest biologists who ever lived, wrote this to me: 'I don't have much to tell you; I'm only a veterinarian.' And you call *me* modest? Give me a break! Bosciàn had understood the mysteries of the cell, the origin of life itself."

The second Bignami, Vittorio, chief organizer inside the Federation, now spoke up. Animate matter and its cells had brought to mind those cells, equally important, that were his daily bread: the party cells of Reggio and the province. The ever-perfectible science of organization was just what he wanted to talk about, and the conversation picked up and became animated. Ferranini saw that he could have been more indulgent with them. He was quite happy to see his two comrades, and besides that, his reputation as a difficult type (utterly honest, true-blue, but hard to know how to deal with, and therefore avoided by many) was one he'd happily have done without. In the end, it was always the politicians who needed politics more than politics needed them.

* * *

Close to 10:00 p.m., as they were getting ready to leave, the owner came to tell the Honorable Ferranini that he was wanted on the phone.

---

10. Alexander Oparin (1894-1980), Soviet biochemist who formulated a then pioneering theory of how life originates from chemical compounds via coacervates, droplets of molecules.

Nuccia? Could it be? It was rare that his friend called him in a public place, even at the trattoria. He had so often warned her to be careful.

But yes, it was Nuccia. She was at the station, waiting for a train, summoned to Milan by her publishing house. They were concerned about the shop. (They had sent her to Rome a few months before to manage a bookstore in the center.) And there were going to be complaints because, it was true, she wasn't selling much, although she had gotten herself sent to Rome promising to salvage a business in trouble. But it was not her fault; the bookstore was a hole, the staff temporary, and Romans didn't read, or else they only read newspapers on the bus, over other people's shoulders.

"It's all right; I can take care of myself. You can be sure they won't budge me from Rome. I'm worried about Giulia; she's in bed with a fever. I got a letter today from my father."

Nuccia was separated from her husband, and her parents looked after her child. A girl of seven. Too young, Nuccia said (quite candidly) for a mother like herself who was "too old."

"It's the flu, I think. In any case, I can't stay away more than two days. Saturday night I'm leaving, and I'll be back here Sunday morning."

"Except for the fact," said Ferranini after hearing her out, "that you can't go because the trains are blocked. There's a rail workers' strike."

He himself had been sent to speak to the Union of Railway Car Workers at Trastevere Station. And Boatta had announced the start of the strike during his speech in the Chamber. Three hours ago.

"No, Walter. The word came in: counterorders, comrades. No strike. I'm here, and the trains are arriving and departing. Unfortunately. I was counting on it."

"That's impossible."

"Surprised, my dear? This is the way things always go for us."

"Come on, you cynic. *Qualunquista*[11]*!*"

"As you like," said Nuccia cheerfully. "But we lack method, decisiveness, toughness. And you know who said that. Gramsci, of course. But also the Man from Predappio[12]."

"Enough foolishness," he said sharply.

There were certain matters Ferranini refused to joke about, and in any case he never joked, about any matter. That Nuccia had a streak of *qualunquismo* was undeniable.

---

11. Politically apathetic, someone who "doesn't give a damn" about ideological consistency.
12. Benito Mussolini.

"Sometimes you lack all sensitivity. You were a partisan. Aren't you ashamed?"

"Sensitivity I have in bed, where it's more useful to you. Ah, listen. I have an idea that you might like. That you 'should' like, rather."

Her voice was low.

"Saturday night, come to sleep with me. You can get the key from the doorkeeper. I made my bed for you with fresh-ironed sheets."

A pause. Was she waiting for him to say, you didn't have to do that?

"I get in at 7:00 a.m.; I'm home at 7:30. I'll just clean up a moment. At quarter to 8:00, you know Walter, we'll be . . . happy. You know?"

It wasn't much. Except that Ferranini was faithful to his habits (so very faithful!) and felt at ease only in his own room, where there were no frills and no heat. Changing beds bothered him; he was no longer young.

"So you don't want to. Oh, Walter."

Ferranini looked around to be sure the phone closet was tightly closed.

"That stuff is for the luxury lovers. Too refined for me."

"What kind of vows did you take to get into the PCI?"

Silence.

"Watch out Walter, you'll lose me."

He laughed, finally.

"No, I won't lose you. Sunday morning I'll be at the station to meet you, and we'll go home right away. We'll take a taxi."

"Well, good thing you're not offering to take me on the bus," said she, knowing he was even more frugal than he was austere.

"Ciao. Think about your daughter."

It was the longest phone call they'd ever had. He put the phone down with a sigh, and relieved, went back to the Bignami cousins. ■

Translated by Frederika Randall

THE PIER'S FLOWERS

Mauro Castellani

Aldo Palazzeschi (1885-1974) was an Italian poet and novelist. Not easily aligned with any particular literary movement, and usually classified as "irregular," early on in his career he was influenced in turn by symbolism, *scapigliatura* (bohemianism), futurism, and the decadent movement of *crepuscolarismo* ("the twilight school"). He remained experimental throughout his creative life, though in the years immediately after WWI—the so-called period of "return to order"—he moved briefly to realism. In the 1960s he enthusiastically embraced the *neoavanguardia*.

Palazzeschi's trademark is his lightheartedness: his art captures the reader with its freshness, playfulness, and spontaneity (*ludus*). Palazzeschi rebels against both classicism and aestheticism, destabilizing with irony, and indeed self-irony, all points of reference: aesthetic, political, moral. Yet his unrestrained but candid irreverence never violates bourgeois common sense and good taste. Palazzeschi mocks the literary tradition with its hallowed symbols (e.g. Hamlet) and its canonical writers, targeting especially poets who exult in the magniloquent and prophetic, and sneers at conformism in poetry as well as academia.

"Melodrama" (1972) and "The Writer" (1972) are from the collection *Via delle cento stelle* 1971-1972, Mondadori, 1972. "To Be or Not to Be" (1968) is from *Cuor mio*, Mondadori, 1968.

MELODRAMA

Aldo Palazzeschi

No doubt the Italian spirit
of recent times
has been forged in the fire of
melodrama.
Melodrama is the mark
of our aged,
and stubborn, civilization.
With this premise in mind
all we do is keep asking:
did a melodramatic Italian language
create melodrama,
or did melodrama render it
melodramatic?

Translated by Katia Pansa

THE WRITER

Aldo Palazzeschi

Writing writing writing . . .
Why does a writer write?
Can we know?
Do we know?
To pursue one career among others?
for the love of something?
Perhaps
for the love of the word
to see it glow
ever more beautiful, bright, enchanting,
he polishes it always
for this alone
without a trace
of vanity?
He writes with the hope
of finding an unknown hand
that he can grasp
in the darkness.

Translated by Katia Pansa

TO BE OR NOT TO BE

Aldo Palazzeschi

Today I thought of you,
Hamlet, you bore,
you made such a fuss
after losing the thread
of real living
in this world
where we struggle
in vain
at times with joy
at others with melancholy
to know who we are
and what it is to live.
Today is a lovely day
for me
everything around is
the color of roses:
joy triumphs.
In these moments
of gladness, of elation
I reply to you:
"I am!"
End of story.

Translated by Katia Pansa

Patrizia Vicinelli (Bologna, 1943–1991) first read publicly in 1966 with the *neoavanguardia* Gruppo 63 and, though not yet twenty-three, she amazed the audience (and her fellow readers), earning immediate praise for her vocal and interpretive gifts.

Vicinelli struggled with drug addiction, endured imprisonment and years as a fugitive in Morocco, and ultimately died a slow death from AIDS—experiences which emerge in her poetry. One critic called her "a kamikaze of experience"; in her life and work, "everything is friction." She favored the *non-sensi* of the great surrealists, and her written work served almost as a score for her improvised performances. Her visual poetry was also exhibited around the world—from Milan to New York, from Tokyo to San Francisco. Her entire oeuvre was collected by Cecilia Bello Minciacchi and published as *Non sempre ricordano: Poesia Prosa Performance* (2009).

The poems included here were written in Rebibbia prison where Vicinelli spent nine months (1977–1978). She was arrested for possession of hashish, but many believed the charges were trumped up in retaliation for her vocal opposition (along with Pasolini, Eco, and Moravia) to the long imprisonment on false charges of the writer Aldo Braibanti. While in prison, she also wrote a reinterpretation of Cinderella featuring dialogues with the character of Cassiopeia, and staged the work with her fellow prisoners.

The following series, *Three poems from Rebibbia Prison* (1977-1978), was published posthumously in *Patrizia Vicinelli, Non sempre ricordano: Poesia Prosa Performance*, edited by Cecilia Bello Minciacchi (Casa Editrice Le Lettere, 2009).

The last poem, "I will not return", was originally published in *codice biancaneve international*, edited by Franco Beltrametti and Dario Villa, no. 0, 1992.

[GOLD RAIN AND LAMENTS]

Patrizia Vicinelli

gold rain and laments and a confusion
of angels however immobile
but they projected them
they needed them
mirror against a summer storm
recalling cataclysms
upheavals
unknown heroes
who gave themselves in a thousand pieces
scattering themselves within every one of us

Translated by Olivia E. Sears

[OH EVIDENCE MOCK ME]

Patrizia Vicinelli

Oh evidence mock me
my untamed unconscious
true *garden* of delights gathered
exploding fertile luminous luminary
finally
light and night and indecipherable depth
silence of universal pastures
the motionless cultivation
in which we live
our reciprocal presences
strolling
in total harmony or
final emergence ultimate resurrection
mirror a familiar tool
now to be tossed away
fertile fields always and
forever
at our disposition.

Translated by Olivia E. Sears

[LIKE BEASTS "THE LIONS"]

Patrizia Vicinelli

like beasts "the lions"
we wait for the meal
at 12 o'clock noon

between one station and the next
menu the same every day of the week
) run towards the guy
with the staff and the grappling hook
the red meat drops down
AND WE EAT IT.
And then with the abomination in our mouths
we must make the drifting hours *fly*,
so at 7 o'clock, hour nineteen,
at the other meal
you can say
"today too has passed"
and another day rolls by,
full of disgust and apathy.

And yet I will not give them proof of what they suspect,
of my unrepentant will.

Only for us, only for you all, do I strive and adapt.
To create fires that last, visible even in the distance.
All this must have some meaning beyond the boundaries of that dementia that is human law. We men and demiurges of our own destiny forever. Being last in this round, elsewhere we are the first, and we face this fatal experience of every avant-garde. Not by our choice. And yet some *thing* enables our will to endure, and the tension that leads in other directions, wanting that human geography already visible in ourselves to be mapped on everyone.
Best to resist, to hold out in this determination. We expect to see others undergo these same trials, others who have a single point of view, the connection that condemns us based on principles with no foundation.

Translated by Olivia E. Sears

I WILL NOT RETURN

Patrizia Vicinelli

I will not return.
Over the burning bridges
of summer
the moon shines
they shine
narrow striped shoes
glimpsed
on deserted frozen piazzas
of winter their neglect
of time could be
a good start
but beneath this atmospheric sense
anguish
I promised
I will never go back there.
I run up against
and I resolve
facing
the fiery abyss
such howling
approaching all alone
to have it
conditioned in the mind
the fractured time
the wasted time
we are on loan
now.
The solitary night clouds
this sound that is already
twentieth century
what are the little pearls doing
they are beading up on us
who sweat sadness
from every pore

what pattern
of unyielding spots.
There would be another path
to take
long difficult impassable
swallowing
to push
down
saliva
bile
bitter pills
that sometimes come along
they come along sometimes.
Notes all deep bass
abysmal decayed
the air is searing
when it burns you
the bitter sun in black.
Pins glimmers
resin
acrid sandalwood incense spreads
everyone
standing
like flowers strung together
in their rise the height
of unfurling
of unfolding.

Translated by Olivia E. Sears

Edoardo Sanguineti (Genoa, 1930—2010) was one of the most important Italian writers, scholars, and intellectuals of the second half of the twentieth century, above all known as a profoundly original poet whose innovations expanded the boundaries of the avant-garde and influenced generations of younger writers in Italy.

He published his first collection of poetry, *Laborintus*, in 1956, when only twenty-six years old. This collection set the stage for Sanguineti's long career as a poetic radical by opposing the mainstream lyric tradition and championing a poetics of fragmentation and dissociation. In 1963, along with Umberto Eco and other writers, Sanguineti founded Gruppo 63, a movement dedicated to the development of new artistic forms.

In the next decade, Sanguineti began to be widely recognized for an enthusiastically cantankerous poetry that subverted conventional aesthetic values and rejected sublimity in favor of a privileging of daily human life. He published more than forty volumes of poetry (*Postkarten, Stracciafoglio, Scartabello, Segnalibro, Codicillo, Rebus, Novissimum Testamentum,* and *Bisbidis*, to name some) and acquired a large and appreciative readership. Although his earliest poetry was difficult and clotted with polyglot density, over the decades his work became more open and direct, exuberant and playful, while never straying from its commitment to radical experimentation in language and form.

"A Novel" is from *Stracciafoglio: Poesie 1977-1979*, Feltrinelli, 1980; "The Ballad of the Wind" is from *Ballate (1982-1989)*, in *Il gatto lupesco. Poesie (1982-2001)*, Feltrinelli, 2002; "*For H.C. (April 1996)*" is from *Poesie fuggitive (1996-2001)*, in *Il gatto lupesco. Poesie (1982-2001)*, Feltrinelli, 2002.

A NOVEL
Edoardo Sanguineti

if one dies of love, then for our part, we are dead:
we are a cheap romantic novel in action: (or better,
a social-realist novel, but cunningly camouflaged as a Harlequin
weeper): (or better yet,
we're a risque bodice-ripper): (a rosé): (no, we are a couple of
dynamic, decaying old dodderers,
squashed in the numbing grip of a silver wedding): (one step away,
barely an inch
from a pitch-black thriller): (or a red romance) and we arouse, to be
honest,
compassion and pity:
here are the coordinates you need: I'm returning from Como,
it's September 26,
9:37 pm, I just asked for the check at the restaurant, I will catch the
express
at 9:50, and I understood you: that's all:
because for you, for me, it's no longer possible
to put up with it, this irresolvable ambivalence, in the wine of the life
that we live:
this life, moreover: (life): (diluted, polluted): and if I tell you and
write to you that
I'm nothing more than a contemporary, we're lucky if 25% of our
natural heirs
can understand me, understand us, in the present state of affairs:
and so, with best wishes, then, let me add, that we:
if one lives of love, we are alive:

Translated by Robert Hahn and Michela Martini

THE BALLAD OF THE WIND

Edoardo Sanguineti

on his head has he crowns times three,
this apostle of Vatican Rome:
he celebrates the cuckold-angel's feast,
but when all of his prayers are consumed,
he ends the way the sacristan ends,
swept away by the blast of ten winds:

white has the great king painted his palazzo
and red has he painted his grand square:
the rockets shaken from his hand sow terror,
but just as his soldiers die, he dies also,
when the final fear and trembling descend,
swept away by the force of a hundred winds:

the baron plays with the bear and the bull,
night and day devours he the labor force:
with green cards is his gullet gorged,
but when his eyes explode with molten gold,
he ends the way a common vagrant ends,
swept off by the rush of a thousand winds:
and whoever fashions sound and speech
whoever sculpts statues and decorates walls,
hungers for the fame he never achieves
but dies snuffed out like anyone at all,
when his psalm blasts him to glory be,
all blown away, both body and memory:

dancing, raging, you all go below
and vanish, wailing, in a black hole:
who leaves most behind suffers most of all,
the worse your sins, the deeper your fall:
creatures of breath, will-o-the-wisps,
see how we dance now, light with delight:

Translated by Robert Hahn and Michela Martini

FOR H.C. (APRIL 1996)

Edoardo Sanguineti

Wald I
and so, my pitiless one, I shyly raise a toast:
the morning cockroach is a newborn dream:
my spiders gesticulate serial dementias,
nuptial words, remaining vague:
in a cunning experiment the ring is crazy,
a brutally zealous worm in the monstrous night:
now in a livid void I must change myself,
scratching out the many bristled mountains:
infernal irons in the skinny little beds,
the merciless spirals atomize me:

Wald II
the trebled cube, crisp and credulous,
minimal, dactylic, is a signifier:
but frenetic she-devils leap about,
naked and gestural pearls, weak from worry:
panting leaves decree dawns,
misty worms, tusks in shifty niches:
a slow dwarf, sprightly and hoarse, bites me,
selecting among the seductive worlds:
ardent wrinkles on wooden masks, desperate,
deny me, at least, my amens:

Wald III
at a hard juncture, inveterate, I fertilize myself:
a sleep is a ribbon, and in its midst is desire:
minimal globe of diseases exposing itself
to my nubile zones of severities, of tapestries:
acidulous forests, amber, aquamarine,
the little ampules are aluminum paws:
a blackish light rules the air here,
irresistible and swift, with a monotonous thirst:
ardent nouns, in my chemical nodes,
scattered zombies, are mythical stones:

Translated by Robert Hahn and Michela Martini

GLORY 04

Rosebud Rosabella

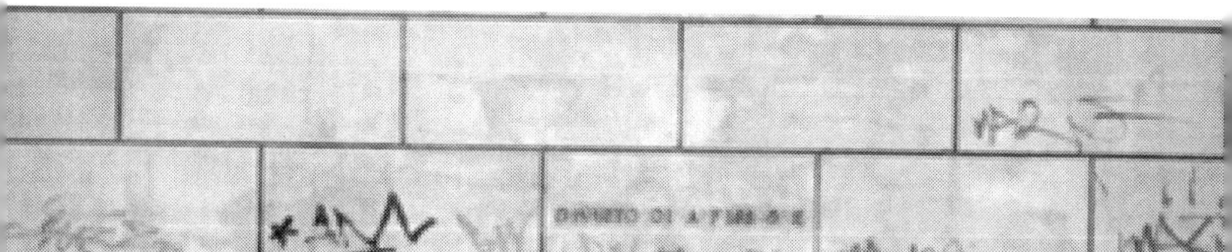

Valerio Magrelli was born in 1957 in Rome. He studied at the Sorbonne (literature and film) and earned a degree in philosophy at the University of Rome. He teaches French literature at the Universities of Pisa and Cassino. He is the author of many scholarly works on French poetry, and of translations of Mallarmé, Valèry, Jarry, Char, and Ponge. His first collection of poetry, *Ora serrate retinae*, came out in 1980 and won the Premio Mondello. His second collection, *Nature e venature* (1987), was followed by *Esercizi di tipologia* (1992) and *Didascalie per la lettura di un giornale* (1999), and, most recently, *Disturbi del sistema binario* (2006). In 2003 he published the novel *Nel condominio della carne*. Magrelli has also won the Premio Letterario Viareggio, 1987, the Premio Librex-Montale, 1992, and the Premio "Feltrinelli" of the Accademia dei Lincei, 2003. He continues to contribute actively to the cultural pages of Italian newspapers and journals.

The following poems are from the collection *Poesie (1980-1992) e altre poesie*, Einaudi, 1996.

[THIS PAGE IS AN UNINHABITED ROOM]

Valerio Magrelli

This page is an uninhabited room.
Every so often I bring in a broken chair
or a pile of newspapers, and I leave them there
in a corner: that's all.
Whatever is left over finds its place here
and settles into the truce from use.
This is the last stop of the objects
before they leave the horizon of the house,
in the bright light of their sunset.

Translated by Margaret Brose

[SOME BOOKS CAN BE USED]

Valerio Magrelli

Some books can be used
to reveal other books
but writing in general is a hiding,
a subtracting from reality something
that you will then miss.
This dialectic of the sign
pointing out things and their pain
teaches us to recognize them.

Translated by Margaret Brose

Giacomo Pilati, a Trapani native, is winner of two Oscar della Televisione Privata Awards as well as the Giuseppe Fava National Journalism Award. Founder of the monthly journal *Lo Scarabeo*, Pilati has published *Le Siciliane* (Coppola, 1998), *Erice la montagna incantata* (Anselmo, 2000), *La cucina trapanese e delle isole - le storie, il lavoro, il cibo* (Muzzio, 2004), *La città dei poveri* (Il Pozzo di Giacobbe, 2006), and *Le altre siciliane* (Coppola, 2008), translated into English as *Sicilian Women* (Legas, 2008). *Minchia di re*, published by Mursia in 2004, was the basis for Donatella Maiorca's 2009 film, *Viola di mare*. His novel, *Sulla punta del mare*, was published by Mursia in 2012. For his cultural efforts in Italy, Pilati earned the title of *Cavaliere* from the president of the Italian Republic in 2012.

The following is an excerpt from *Minchia di re*.

THE KING'S COCK

Giacomo Pilati

The Donzella di mare is a hermaphroditic fish.
In many parts of Sicily, when it passes into its
masculine phase, they call it "The King's Cock."

Author's Preface

A forgotten scandal resurfaces. It was an old wives' tale, a part of a documentary film hidden between the islands of the Mediterranean. It becomes a torment, caught up in truth, legend, and lies. It gives me no respite.

Garibaldi and his Mille had just landed in Italy. National unity was unfolding in dramatic, yet hopeful, events. On a small island, one woman waged an even greater revolution: in order to survive the scandal of her own homosexuality she decided to pass herself off as a man. At the age of twenty-five she became another person: wearing a cap, cigar in mouth, a well-off family, and enough power to hide the absurd transformation.

I gather accounts, I dig in archives. And in the end I find it. A yellowed piece of paper. Four lines telling the story of one day in a life: that day. It's all true. She really existed. And then she became he. Now I know who I'm talking about. I follow that body. I invent a life for her. So that she won't be dead any longer, really, to give her the life I want her to have. This is the story of the true event of a metamorphosis, the rest is pure invention.

I

Huge stars like fireworks flared in the sky and there must have been a moon that night. A full moon that impregnates the sea urchins, filling them with eggs, a moon that stuns the sperm and fastens it to the urchins' bellies before the tide rolls out again. My father wanted a son. Only a son for the overseer of the tufa mines of Cala Tramontana. A girl was women's work, anyone could have a girl. And shame is worse than death for a man of this sort. He held a knife to her throat as she gave birth, the bastard.

"It better be a man like me. If it's a girl, I swear I'll kill you."

A scream drawn out infinitely, choked back in the belly and thrown out like a snake slithering across the stones, followed by the thin reed of a child. That's my mother there, a child herself of fifteen. She's got the edge of the pillow between her teeth, a single tear trickles down her cheek like a spring that ends in a mud puddle. My mother, who doesn't know how to scream, my mother, who lacks the strength to talk back to my father, it's for God to decide. Scream, mamma, I beg you, at least now, let me hear your voice, make me love your desperation that cannot always be condemnation. Redeem your shame. Take that knife from your throat, grab his wrist, you could stab him in the heart in the wink of an eye. This way your silence and your anguish will be your liberation. Now, mamma. Silence. I am born. Red and slimy, like a lump of jelly, a big shrimp like the ones that set the fishermen on fire. My father hasn't seen anything yet. He doesn't want to know. Tell him I'm a girl. I am born. A girl, Papa. And you didn't kill Mamma. Resign yourself to me. I am Pina. That's the way I was born. And, I swear, the moon was full.

II

Nicolino's father is Mastro Paolo, my father's right hand man in the mines. His house is in the country. Since we have a bicycle we've got the time to stop for a drink at Zucco's water fountain. I'm the one seated on the crossbar, with the skirt down to her ankles that's clipped on with clothespins and pantaloons that make me want to laugh. I've got short hair and thick, black eyebrows like two brushes, my legs tucked up above the pedals, my head under Nicola's head and away from the wind. I can see now those jumps that made my head spin and made me close my eyes so I wouldn't fall. Beneath us the sea, who doesn't care if we're there or not. The sea that's always there and has no need of us to know it's alive. But here we are and there lies the sea. Marvelous. We who tread the rocks of the sheep track high above the island's deepest abyss, we who stop and linger to watch it, to throw stones at it to see who's the best and can throw them the farthest. To see who knows how to make little skips on its surface. We run at the sea, we breathe in its breath, its color. And we hold it in even while on land, with the horizon and its boats that slip down on us. We who are thirteen and who knows how old the sea is.

There, over there is Nicolino's house. Just another bit and we've arrived. These last few yards smell of wild grass, of sweat, of cheese. Of sheep's cheese, for certain. Just one more push, pump your legs just a bit more. A dash to the stable, the stall at the end. Here we are. With our hands dirty from dry donkey shit. Add a little straw, give it a nice shake, add a grape leaf, one of those big ones and you're done. The cigarette is ready. We make two, three at a time. Then we let them dry for three days. Each time the smoke swells in your chest and then hits your head like a wallop it's a discovery. We're sitting outside leaning against the stable wall, and the smoke disappears as we gaze at the sea that stretches out beneath our feet. The sea that jumps on the cliff like someone crazed, as if all the rest, the pines, the strawberry trees, the prickly pear, were nothing. As if they weren't there. Because the sea has beaten them, and they have decided not to follow it as it falls back into freedom. They've raised their arms, they've given in. You go ahead then, since you can crash the rocks, split the shadows and do what you want with them. We can't, we'll stay behind you here on shore and die. But we'll leave you the perfume of our sap just for love.

I look on the plants as they discuss this with the sea. I don't meet the eyes that follow me. Like that spy Bastiano Tortorici, *'u picararu*, who can't keep anything to himself. And my father who sent him. My father is two meters of cloth. His beard and hair make his face longer and there in the middle are his eyes, straight like two sentinels. Below this, his nose pointing at me. And the thin mouth, like a crack in a terracotta statue. A sharp blade that slices my skin. His arms are crossed. He doesn't speak, it's his nose that calls me. He lowers it and it's like a finger that moves. I am before him. I don't even have the time to look him in the eye. I feel my cheek flame like fireworks over the mountain. He's afire, as if attacked by an octopus. With his tentacles still moving as he shuts the door behind him. The tirade arrives like wind that rattles the windows. "Smoking is for *buttane*, for whores. Shameless girl. If I see you doing it I'll kill you."

He has no mercy for the other two women in our house. Agnese is my mother's sister. She was supposed to enter the convent at Santo Spirito. But you had to go into town and she'd never been off the island. So she became her own sort of nun. She sewed a long dark brown habit and she wears a dark brown kerchief, a crucifix, sandals.

And with all her might she drove inside her own beauty so that now it's dying within her. And my mother, a sainted woman. Always ready to forgive. Prayers, kitchen, needlework. Never one word too many, never an untimely sigh. With her heart simmering all day, from morning to night. So when night arrives it's a dried fig at the bottom of a tree, sticky with leaves and dirt.

This time my father did things the right way. He took four lengths of wood and nailed them across my windows. This way I can't leave the house, I can't escape. I feel the nails root under my skin, find my bones. My mother brings me food, her eyes lowered. She doesn't speak, she says nothing. Nor any word every evening when my father roars and curses the men that come asking for work in the mines. And he bellows that there's not enough work for everyone, and that he calls workers when he's got a mind to. My father who appears in the doorway of the house with dogs that haven't been fed and drops the leash if those poor men get down on their knees and beg him for a kilo of flour, for a plot of land.

"Maybe just for a month, Mastro Nino, seeing that my children are hungry. And since the fishing season is a ways off."

And my father who shuts the door, leaving them outside, abandoned to their own miserable meals of sardines with a little spit and a bed that makes you cry and curse the day you were born.

My mother, now that I look at her, is thirty years old. She goes into the storeroom, with a cup of water and a crust of hard bread. Her eyes are lowered, she's ashamed. She knows that none of this makes any sense, that there's no reason for it. And she buries this within her, like a belly-ache. Now the cup is on the wooden stool, she's turned, she hasn't looked at me. She's gone.

III

It's a beautiful sunny morning above Long Island. The piazza, with its golden brown stones facing the sea, is ready to weigh anchor and set sail. Fifi the mute, as blond as a Norman, is on the dock repairing fishing nets. He's kneeling, bent over the mesh. He looks at the Burrutos' palace and he makes the sign of the cross three times. The Burrutos are masters of everything you see. He eats their bread. And that bread is blessed by God. They are God.

Sara is the daughter of the palace caretaker. The owners are on the island five months out of the year. They come for the sardine season and they go back to town at the end of autumn. But this year they have stayed longer. And Mario Fascella's daughter has a little more time to stay in the piazza and watch Fifi the mute mend the nets. When the baron Luigi Burruto is on the island he doesn't like children underfoot. So the caretaker dispatches his three children and lets them roam the streets until sundown.

I fell in love with her eyes. Green like the streams inside the grotto at Minnola, with her breasts round as eggplants with nipples pointy like green olives. And her mouth, two bruised mulberry leaves. Skin so white that she looks like an angel, skin that never sees the light of day. The sun cannot penetrate it. For me, this is what angels are like. And she is. Still, watching Fifi. Me too. I feel her skin brushing me. Without guilt. I feel a shiver inside me. I'm feverish. What's happening to me? I feel my breath keeping time with my heart. There's an animal inside me. Her lips are so close. I can smell her breath. It smells of musk, of citronella, of a damp sparrow. I want the taste of that breeze in my body. I feel a great heat within me. What it can be, I don't know. But I feel good. Her eyes are two blue pools of water that shimmer on the top of the mountain in the meadows by the castle and reflect the sky, the sun, the dark. For her I am that dark. She doesn't want to be here with me. On this spring afternoon, with the fishing boats docked next to each other in the port. She'd like to be in the garden at the baron's villa, hidden among the trees where no one can see her. And to become air so she can play with the wooden trains and tricycle of her master's son, without really existing. The water caresses the sand, the stones slowly move in the tide. They turn in the water, sink, float to the surface, and sink once more. The stones' sound that I hear break against other stones, that I hear break the surf. And there they are, lapping in the water, then drip-drying. To die in the sun. My hand is still, my breath, too. Only the stones speak. I breathe out.

"You're as beautiful as an angel."

And I say it without thinking. My heart in a state, I'd rather not have this fever that *femmine*, like me, have. But I have this desire in my throat and I can't stop it, and it makes me speak, honey in my voice.

"Are you crazy? It's a sin to say so."

"What's a sin?"

Sara dangles her head. "It's something you don't say because you can't do it."

And she runs away, taking my turmoil with her.

IV

The castle is a rotted-out lump perched for who knows how long on the toothless gums of the island. It's at the very top of a carbuncle of land, far down where the earth plays with the sea when no one's looking. Federico's castle is a prison. I know that now, but for a long time I thought there were monsters inside, damned souls, men with the heads of serpents and feet of pigs. They light fires on the beach. All day they gather wood to mark the feast of the Madonna of the Mines. The rosaries, the wrinkled hands that count the olive pits painted red, and then everyone down on the beach yelling "Viva Maria, viva Maria," their eyes filled with smoke and ash, untethering the rage they have inside. Even my mother and my aunt, whom my father, for once, leaves alone. That's why they say that the women in the house of the overseer of the Cala Tramontana quarry are so religious.

It seemed like nighttime to me, but it must have really been evening. Nicolino and I met at Senzapatri beach; this is the one time all year that we can do what we want until midnight with the excuse that we're gathering wood for the Madonna. We haven't really realized it, but we've practically reached the castle. The hot southern wind, *libeccio*, blows and I can feel the grass move, I feel it grow beneath me. Nicolino is scared, his heart beating like a drum when he sees that we've gone all the way up the mountain. But I'm curious, I want to see what's inside, I want to look these monsters in the face. I can't live my whole life looking at the sky above my part of the island without seeing what it looks like over here, on that hump of an animal that's mortally wounded. Nicolino hears someone coming toward us, turns and is gone like a flash of lightning in the clear heavens when the light strafes the sky outlining the silver wound. And even if these monsters tear me limb from limb, what would it change? No one would ever know that I existed, that I was, that I exist. So I just stand still, motionless, and wait to see the monster. My eyes are cast down. I raise them. There it is, before me. With one foot on a stone and the other in midair. It's an old man with white hair, soldier's boots, a shirt made out of an old sack, the same for his pants.

"Who are you?"

"I heard a noise. Like an animal in need. It's easy to catch a paw in the thorns around here."

"And that's what happened. Good girl."

"Liar. You're an old man."

"I'm an animal in need."

"What do you need?"

"Some company."

"Are you from somewhere else?"

"I live in the castle."

"So you're a soldier."

"I'm a prisoner."

I don't understand, I'm confused. Who is this old man who has suddenly appeared before me? The moon shows only half his face. He could be the same age as Fifi the mute, or Nicolino's grandpa. His eyes are the blue of the drawings the baron's children hang in the garden for the feast of Saint Theresa. A cross high on a dark oval. Behind it the sky is a blue so beautiful I haven't ever seen its like here. And beneath it there they are, the baron's children, on their knees praying to their pieces of paper.

"Why don't you run away? You don't wear leg irons and your hands are free, too."

"I can't, I told you, I'm a prisoner."

"So what are you doing outside the castle then?"

"I'm going to take a dip, down there in the lagoon."

"There are leeches in there. Nobody goes in."

"That's why I do. They stick to my skin and suck my blood. One good pluck and they're in my sack."

"But they're no good to eat."

"I offer them to the soldiers at the castle. If you're sick and you wear a uniform, they'll bleed you. But if one of us inmates takes sick they let us die."

"That's terrible."

"When I'm in with the leeches I have no master. I can think what I want, horses with three heads, goats that fly. If I move a little I can see the sea. And the mold and the coal don't suffocate me."

"Yes, but you get hurt."

"Everything has its price."

I can already see the first of the fireworks. A race along the sheep track. I hurdle boulders, my heart beating faster and faster, my breath roaring in my ears. The stones skitter beneath my shoes. I fall, no, I make it. I can't stop myself. I look at the moon diving into the sea. I quickly reach the outline of the pines, they run by my side. I'm the one who can't control her legs. Nothing can stop me. The fireworks there beneath me. My father will be looking for me. My mother will be clamping her lips together not knowing what to say. I have arrived. My shoulders ache, savaged by the wood I tied to my back. Just a little bit more and there I am on the Senzapietri beach. Nothing has happened. I see his back over there, he hasn't looked for me. My mother comes right up to me.

"You wretch. Your father thinks that you weren't allowed to come as punishment. Thank God he believed it. This is no hour to be running around."

"I went to the castle."

"To the castle?"

"To get wood."

"You must be missing a part. A girl with good sense doesn't go looking for trouble."

"But I did it for Our Lady."

"Go home right away. And don't let your father see you until tomorrow."

V

I next see Sara up the mountain. Her shepherd dog is with her, white and all muddy. The next time I see her we have already sworn in silence that our eyes won't seek each other's, that we will say no more those words that scratch at the soul and reveal things no one wants to find. I have a knife in my hands. I'm bent over cutting wild grass, *burannia* and *gira*. My lord and master wants the tender grass with all its roots because he says that you can smell the first autumn rains in the earth that clings to them. But I collect it for my mother's sake. So that when he comes home at night he doesn't ask her what she's done, doesn't rummage through the garbage to look for proof of the thing she's done wrong. The apple core thrown away with some fruit still on it. A piece of moldy bread. Every night, boiled *gira* and *burannia*. Down the hatch chasing a liter of wine. He throws himself into bed without a word to anyone. And we are safe.

But right now all that counts is Sara before me. I pretend not to look at her. I hold a staff in my hands. A hemp sack across my chest, my hair done up in my cap. A shirt with some lace bits that must have been my aunt's before she became a nun. The noise of the feast of Saint John arrives from afar. Mandolins and accordions, glasses of wine and new clothing. And she is so beautiful. The curls fall on her shoulders, forming triangles, squares. One shape inside of another. Her golden hair fogs my brain. It sews my mouth shut. Yes, her mouth, the one I'd like to fix my lips to. Committing no sin. For pleasure only. I am inside of her, with my eyes planted on the surface of her heart, on the tiniest bit of flesh that I can wrest from her. I set my sack down on a stone so it won't get muddy. The dog comes toward me and she after him. She stands before me. Her skin is giving off the same heat as before. My eyes strain to drink her in, all of her just as she is, wholesome. To eat her, digest her, hide her deep inside me. Sara and I stand close to each other. The dog barks, the sack on the ground is full of *gira* and *burrania*. I run away. No. I embrace her. She is mine. There is no arguing. There is only this passion, this heat that takes me and that I don't know how to resist. I caress her face, wind my fingers in her hair. She is before me, motionless. Then suddenly she kisses me. She is but a small shadow on my lips that enters my throat. We grab hands and tumble dizzyingly down the hill with the dog behind us. We jump ditches, we hover atop the stones. With our hearts filled with each other. There's a weary horse in my chest. I stop, I throw myself on the ground. She is beside me. Her head framed by the backdrop of the sky. A big carruba tree filters the rays of a pale and feeble sun. And we beneath it, blades of bittersweet grass between our teeth. Our hands shake, the wind picks up.

"Let's make a pact."

"Whatever you want."

"Let's swear never to breathe a word of this to anyone."

"It will be our secret."

"Cross your heart we'll never part?"

"Cross my heart."

"Now you belong to me and me to you."

"But we're two girls . . ."

"But we want each other like a boy and a girl."

"I'm afraid we've been seized by a terrible sickness."

"Let's hope we never get better."

With the stars shining above us we float all the way to the piazza, not even aware when we have reached it. The feast of San Giovanni enfolds us into a mass of flesh that draws us into the island's very viscera.

I say to Sara as a sort of joke that I want to have my future told. What with all that's floating on this sea of air and water it won't be hard for the *ciraulo*, the sooth-sayer, to find it. The *ciraulo* is standing on a wooden stool. He's got pomade in his hair and on his mustache, too. His skin must have been soft and smooth once, now his wrists and arms are leather. Every so often he bends, touches his toes with his fingers and his muscles swell like warm ricotta. The *ciraulo* descends from his stool. He goes toward a sack and pulls out drawings with the faces of the saints. He takes them one by one and nails them to the door of his booth. He kneels. Our Fathers. Ave Marias. A woman who must be his wife passes him a jar she took from the saint sack. He unscrews the lid and draws out a live grass snake, so black and narrow he could throw it among lions. And he puts it to graze on his chest, the hairs like bushes black as sea urchins. And he doesn't flinch even when he draws from the same jar a spider as big as his hand that he puts on his shoulder to keep the snake company. Saint Paul is above him, protecting him and helping him grab hold of fate with his own hands and bring it to us poor wretches. These animals that he carries with him are the stigmata of his strength. If he commands the snakes, his gift is as plain as clear water. The first thing he sees are our feelings, he opens them and holds them in his hand like the town patriarch does with the Christ child.

We line up behind his wife even before she has the time to say, "Step right up ladies and gentlemen."

"Who called you?"

"No one, Mastro Ciraulo, we want . . ."

"Get along now, if you can't pay there is no piper."

"But we beg you, Mastro Ciraulo."

"What's in the bag?"

"Bitter greens, lemons and fruit."

"Nuccia, take this sack. Let's see what we can do. Be seated."

I feel my blood stirring and it seems like I can also feel Sara's and that it's the same for her.

"I will read the stars for only one of you."

He looks deep into my eyes. Then Sara's. Then mine again.

"Take tight hold of my hand. Close your eyes and heave a heavy sigh."

He stops for a moment. With his wide eyes staring between me and Sara, his mouth open. From outside there's the sound of people amusing themselves and no one knows how much time passes.

He opens those eyes that want to gobble you up. That are two mirrors in which we can see each other.

"Get along. Take back your things. I don't want any of it. I'm tired and the clouds have covered the stars. Nuccia, bring the sack."

"But we want to know . . ."

"There's nothing to be done."

"But at least one thing . . ."

"Can't do it. Tonight Saint Paul is in a mood for fun."

XXIII

He enters slowly and stops before me like a dog that catches a whiff of wild game. I am crouched in a ball in my lair. His breath rises like steam and a cloud of smoke and dust frames his face. Against the light he is a papier-maché silhouette pasted on the darkness. His steps make the pebbles screech underfoot, his hand shakes me from the torpor of my resignation. I raise my head and then lower it again on the cushion.

"I'm letting you out." He grabs me by the shirt. "I said I'm letting you out."

I see him by lantern light that shows his face like the island's mountains, all crags and crannies.

"You have the priest to thank. He's the one who made me see it's better for everyone if I leave you alone."

"I'm not marrying Ventura."

"Ventura? Who said anything about Ventura? He's back in Tunisia. No, you're not marrying him any more. But you have to do what I tell you to do. You're becoming a man."

"But how can I when everyone knows I'm a girl?"

"I told you you're becoming a man. Women's clothes don't work. Isn't that right?"

"That's right," and I sit with my legs crossed. A hand on the stone wall, he sits down in front of me.

"I'm old and I can't go down in the mines forever. So you're becoming a man and taking my place. I've already talked to the baron."

"But everyone knows I'm a girl."

"No one will say anything. I'll make you the boss right away. Do you see? They won't have the time to think about it before they'll have to say to you 'God save you, Your grace' and 'Your servant.' Do you see?"

"No."

"Do you know what will happen when I'm gone if you stay neither fish nor fowl? The attack dogs will tear you apart, they'll seize your house and you'll finish without a penny."

"What do I have to do?"

"Here are some men's clothes. Put them on and when you're ready we'll go see the bishop, who's coming to the island tomorrow just for this. The baron and the doctor will declare that you are a man and you will be born again."

"But no one will believe it."

"We'll make sure everything is in order. Before the law you will be Pino. That fool Padre Pantaleo made a mistake when he didn't see the balls and prick you've got between your thighs."

"But that's not right. I'm a girl."

"Here everyone thinks what I want them to think. If tomorrow I decide to howl because I've become a dog, I'll make everyone bark."

"What if I said I don't want to dress like a man because I like it fine the way I am."

"You're old enough to decide for yourself. Why ruin your life? I'm letting you out of here anyway, I already swore to God I would. I'll put you on a boat and leave you out at sea."

"I need to think about it."

"I don't think you understand. This is the only thing you can do to save face on the island."

"What's the island got to do with it?"

"My legs don't work the way they used to and the baron knows it. Once I'm gone he'll close the mines. And what will happen to these poor wretches who eat only because I give them bread? They'll starve."

"You starve them now. It's better for them if you go; that way no one will steal their money."

"I just take the extra since they wouldn't know what to do with it. Are there cafés on the island? Taverns? There's nothing. And they don't know what to do with the extra the baron gives them."

"And what do you do with it?"

"I buy land and houses. And they sleep in them. If it weren't for me they'd sleep with the mules in their stalls."

"They pay you to sleep in the houses you stole from them."

"They wouldn't be able to buy a house even if they worked two lifetimes."

"But you steal their money."

"I take what's owed me for giving everyone work."

"But what are you going to do with houses and land? What are you going to do?"

"Money is the oars that row the boat. The baron keeps the mines open, I make them yield, the workers have a roof over their heads and soup in the evening. Everyone's happy."

"But we're not happy."

"This is women's talk. Men like us don't look for happiness, we look for power. Over women, over workers, maybe even over God."

"What's He got to do with it?"

"Oh yes, power even over God. We pray because we want Him near when we're in need. He helps us and we light candles in church and carry Him through the streets once a year. But He helps us because we're strong. And since He does what we want, we're stronger than He is, because we have put Him in service to us."

My lord and master walks away in a cloud of smoke from the lantern. In his absence I unfurl, like a flower whose petals open at night to release the scent it's kept away from the sun, and gathers the essence of the night smelling of citronella, wax, and slumber. My lungs ache from being underground, the sickle of the moon and the sun like a ball far overhead, curled up like an animal in this cave and left to guess about the noises in the house overhead and to distill the words.

I can take no more. If I must die, then at least it will be outside of here, prisoner of a different body that will in some way still be mine. O God, send me a beautiful dream so that tomorrow I can go with a smile to have my head cut off and be given another. I'd like a dream about warriors. Me with a white horse and a sword crossing meadows that are red, yellow, and brown. In a far away olive grove I reach a house made all of glass and there I find Sara, dressed as I am. I take off my armor and she hers. We embrace, we clasp each other tight, our sighs allow no words. A beautiful dream, sweet Saint Patrick, a beautiful dream.

XXIV

The bishop's lower lip looks like the chute they send the blocks of tufa down when loading the ships. He is shorter than I am, fat, and virtually bald. He is wearing a red cassock cut in half by a violet sash around his hips and he's stuffed between the arms of a red velvet chair that I swear was built with him sitting in it. Swinging against his belly, his crucifix looks as if it's alive. He is seated at the end of a long hall draped in white and sky blue silk. On the ceiling, angels with round faces and wings where they should have ears cover Our Lady's blue mantle. My lord and master brought me with his own carriage. He held the reins as I sat there straight in my trousers, shirt and *cilecco*. He didn't say a word when he saw me. But my mother did. With pain in her voice she said, "I couldn't lose you."

And I said, "Male or female, I will always be your daughter."

She held me tightly in her arms and squeezed me like a lemon as I stroked her hair. And we began to cry. With the tears running down her cheeks she cut my hair. With every handful that fell to the floor I felt one wound open and another close. The swirl of falsehoods and the plotting cut short by the shears.

"Come in my son, come in and don't be afraid."

The windows are so long that I can see the entire mountainside. The deep shadow makes it seem like evening and drives back the light of a day that's barely an hour old.

"You are Pino. Father Angelo has said many wonderful things about you. It could be that even the baron has spoken well of you."

"I am your servant, Your Eminence."

"You are an important person. I am told that many of the island's children depend upon you."

"I am just a sinner, Your Eminence. The worst of sinners."

"That you are lively, restless. They have also said this about you. But not cruel. And you have a pure heart."

"As Your Blessed Eminence wishes."

"Do you know why I have come here today?"

"No, Your Eminence."

"Last night Our Lord spoke to me about you."

"And what did He say?"

"That because of a foolish priest you've been held prisoner in a body that is not your own."

"This is the truth, Your Eminence."

"And I have come to liberate you."

"To put all matters in order."

"We come to the side of those in fear. That is why I am here today."

"And are you afraid, Your Eminence?"

"Come closer. Like this. Yes, I am very afraid of making a mistake. But Our Lord is close by to lend a hand. You love Our Lord, do you not?"

"Your Eminence, if you allow it, I would like to tell you how I feel."

"Speak, my son, speak."

"Respectfully, I feel like Our Lord before His resurrection."

"What are you saying?"

"Before returning to heaven Jesus was dead and he may have asked himself 'What if I am not God?'"

"The Resurrection is a marvelous mystery with many meanings that you are too ignorant to understand. It is difficult even for me and I am His servant."

"But for me it is not so complicated. Listen, Your Eminence. He died on the cross and waited three days before recognizing that He was God. During these three days He was dead. Dead, you see? Like my grandfather, like his grandfather, like Cecè. I am like that. I am dead and now thanks to your blessing I will begin to live."

"It is a great joy, my son."

"It could be that I have been dead for but a moment, or three days, or ten years. This is how I feel, Your Eminence."

"I see, I see. I bless you in the name of the Father, the Son, and the Holy Ghost. You are now Pino with your life ahead of you. I ask only one thing."

"Ask of me anything, Your Eminence."

"You must behave with decorum, you must not be impulsive. You must never make me regret the blessing I have given you. A *masculo* through and through."

"Of course. I give you my word. I give you both: my word as a woman and as a man. May I ask you something, Your Eminence?"

"Of course, my son, we are alone."

"Do you believe Father Pantaleo made a mistake when I was born?"

"As a bishop I believe it, as a man I know the truth. On one hand, the Last Supper and Judas the traitor. On the other, tangles and snarls that I cannot understand. But all it takes is a step backward to see in the story the greatness of God's design. Now go, my son. And may God always bless you." ■

Translated by Ellen Nerenberg

Biancamaria Frabotta was born in Rome in 1946, where she currently lives. She is a professor of contemporary Italian literature at the University of Rome, La Sapienza. She was an active member of the Italian Feminist Movement in the 1970s and 1980s and continues to be a prolific writer of prose, poetry, and plays, as well as critical studies of contemporary Italian poets.

Frabotta has been a contributor to journals and newspapers such as *Nuovi argomenti, aut-aut, Horizonte, Il manifesto, L'Espresso*, and to programming on the RAI. Frabotta's novel *Velocità di fuga* (Reverdito, 1989) was awarded the Premio Tropea in 1989. In 1995 she was awarded the Premio Montale for her volume of poetry *La viandanza* (1982-1992) (Mondadori, 1995). In 2003 *La pianta del pane* (Mondadori, 2003) received four awards: the Premio Lericipea, Premio Dessì, Premio Casentino, and Premio al Comune di Trabia, Palermo. Frabotta's most recent collection, *Da mani mortali* (Mondadori, 2012), was a finalist for the 2012 Strega Prize in poetry.

"[O deceitful sleep who reawakens]" and "[I dream of the Muses of the other hemisphere]" are from *La pianta del pane*; "Post Coitum Test" is from *La viandanza*.

[O DECEITFUL SLEEP WHO REAWAKENS]

Biancamaria Frabotta

O deceitful sleep who reawakens
the unflowered bulbs of the freesias
deep down, between herbs and disturbances
the crocuses replanted in the shadows
offspring of the vainest Narcissus
yellow-hearted, and empty-faced
take me to Paradise *for a couple of hours.*[1]

Translated by Margaret Brose

Translator's Note:

1. In italics in the original; from a Venetian children's lullaby

[I DREAM OF THE MUSES OF THE OTHER HEMISPHERE]

Biancamaria Frabotta

I dream of the Muses of the other hemisphere
goddesses of those who sleep upside down.
In the wide sack of the sky, for example,
the ridge-edge of the waves
wood gathered while still green
white magpies balanced on barbed wire fence.
It takes only a few febrile ideas, it seems,
to halt the thoughts. Only a few stories turned upside down.
Cotton-candy sheep, rising up again, re-counted.

Translated by Margaret Brose

POST COITUM TEST

Biancamaria Frabotta

I made a vow and wrapped myself in a void
but nothing could get through to
that splendid senseless uterus
that dark empty funnel that so
strenuously resists
the loving headlong fall of your little tail
strutting like a peacock.
Ejaculate clear, viscosity normal.
And yet the reaction proved alkaline
but the vitality spent in that hard hour
rose up again, and still endures…
Imagine; such a beautiful baby could have been born.
Instead, as if it were a serpent
needing to be domesticated
a long whistle of wind in the rough seas of the womb
blocked your blond boast of generation.

Translated by Margaret Brose

DREAM ON THE WALL

Mauro Castellani

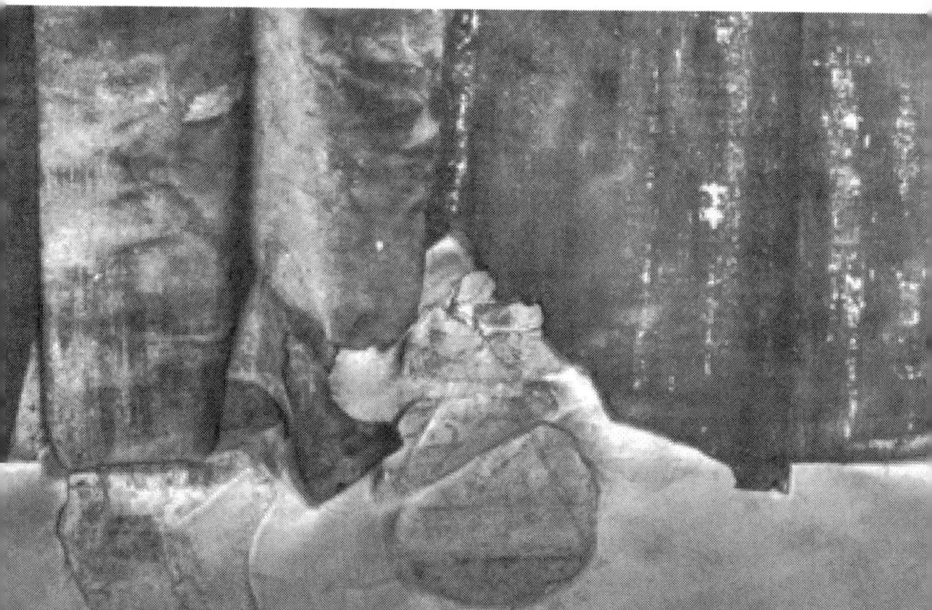

Emanuele Trevi (Rome, 1964) is a literary critic and a writer. He has curated the edition of several works by Italian and French classic and contemporary authors (Alexandre Dumas, Charles Perrault, Emilio Salgari, Giacomo Leopardi, Edmondo De Amicis, Enrico Manganelli, etc.). His book *Istruzioni per l'uso del lupo* (Castelvecchi, 1994), advocating a change in the artificial, technical language of Italian literary criticism was groundbreaking and very positively received. Trevi contributes regularly to newspapers such as *il manifesto, La Stampa, la Repubblica,* is one of the editors of the prestigious literary magazine *Nuovi Argomenti,* and has hosted the cultural radio program Lucifero for RAI Radio 3. His debut novel appeared in 2003 (*I cani del nulla,* Einaudi) and was followed by *Senza verso* (Laterza, 2005), *L'onda del porto* (Laterza, 2005), *Il libro della gioia perpetua* (Rizzoli, 2010), and *Qualcosa di scritto* (Ponte alle Grazie, 2012).

The following is an excerpt from *L'onda del porto*.

THE STAR OF DEJECTION

Emanuele Trevi

Tout ce qui est incompréhensible ne laisse pas d'être
—Pascal

Throughout the month of December, the month of the tsunamis and the massive devastations in Asia, a thick, consistent rain had been falling on Rome, night after night, until the first uncertain gleam of dawn—more like the obstinate, senseless and repetitive monologue of a paranoid god, dazed by ancient resentment, than a mere weather phenomenon. On the pages of newspapers across old, damp, inhospitable Europe, maps were covered with the dark, swollen symbols of clouds from which little circles of snow or the dotted line of storms, often accompanied by the arrows of lightning, stuck out. These zigzags could make you think, after some minutes contemplating the weather forecast, of nose-diving snakes assaulting the earth to avenge some fugitive human misfit. Sometimes these marks resembled bad thoughts, unpleasant memories suddenly resurfacing, breaking through the protective cover of forgetfulness. With my head leaning against the window glass, and my mood *rainier* night after night, I would look for hours at the street lamp hanging above the deserted crosswalk near my house. The night moved slowly, as if stupidly proud of its simulation of eternity. Not once since I began to write, for myself or for my readers, have I had what you could call a good idea, or even something interesting to write about. And yet to think that at least since I was fourteen, I have tried to do nothing else but write, every single day.

It seems the substance of my life is too obtuse, too internal, too self-cancelling for something inside it to have the shape of a meaningful story with a beginning and an end. As an individual, I lack both static and dynamic qualities—and my ability to imagine things has been withering since I was a child. I can't grasp the links of consequence among actions, the infinite and multifarious mating positions—a real kamasutra—that connect cause and effect. My endless personal adventure is so repetitive, so deprived of dramatic turns of event and change of perspective, in sum of any direction, upward or downward, that not even a great romantic novelist, a new Robert Louis Stevenson of misadventures, could pull a compelling subject out of it. It has been a while now since I stopped wondering why every kind of lifeless object, from the simplest to the most complicated, that belongs to me or is within the scope of my temporary jurisdiction, breaks, jams, irreparably deteriorates, in other words somehow stops working as if prey to a suicidal crisis. My things remind me of those nice, wise, prudent mice that at some point decide, entirely on their own, to run towards the coast and happily drown together in the waters of Northern seas. Keys break turning in the keyhole, mufflers corroded by rust detach from vehicles, carburetors flood, pens hemorrhage ink, refrigerators leak water, closet doors detach from their hinges, zippers get stuck, light bulbs burn out, toilet bowls clog up, couch springs give up, vacuum cleaners stop vacuum cleaning, tables shake, cups crack, vinyl records jam. Very trivial facts, these, and about which, individually, there wouldn't be much to say. It's their daily frequency and multiplication that defies any statistic and any attempt of a rational explanation. For a while now I have been keeping a sort of a *record of malfunctions* whose completeness, in any case, leaves much to be desired. I almost consider this record my will, the compulsory report to deliver with shaky hands to the ironic and suspicious angel that blocks the doors of heaven (I can imagine this angel leaning with elegant, cruel nonchalance at the jamb of the door, with a shiny blade of grass hanging from his lips, the long fingers of a hand playing with his perfect curls), questioning the newcomers on how they spent their life, what they learned from it, how they possibly treasured it. The days when absolutely nothing breaks are very rare. And yet, those aren't days that I would describe, in every aspect, as the lucky ones. On the contrary, it's exactly on those days, with the cruel and deaf inflexibility of the moon's phases and of the tides, that the Major Damages brew in the shadows, growing rust and tearing apart seals, ungluing, unscrewing, cracking, charring, short-circuiting—and in every way hurrying silently, obstinately towards the breakdown point, the much-desired ending of the Acclaimed Breakage.

Like watchtowers evenly distanced from one another along surrounding walls, the Major Damages confer rhythm and variety to the Chinese Wall of daily malfunctions, the innumerable *suicides* and likewise innumerable *suicide attempts* of my things. It's in any case among the ranks of the Major Damages that the Penances hide and ripen. This further subdivision shouldn't seem to the patient and friendly reader excessively contorted. Penance is the acme, the initiation secret, the deepest and most cabalistic level of the obscure alphabet of damages. By nature these Penances are rare, but can last several weeks, if not entire months. Indeed they simply consist of the *prolonged* breakage state of certain objects, which refuse to resume functioning, even after having been entrusted to the care of the mechanic, the plumber, the electrician, or any other type of *expert* on the damage in question. Towards all *experts*, I will add incidentally, I harbor an *awe* that easily strays into the pathological, servile, Oedipal realm. It's for this reason that the failure of any expert towards the Penance, temporary or permanent as it may be, doubles in me the bewilderment, the voiceless sorrow, the ancestral fear brought about by a breakdown.

* * *

All in all, rhetoric aside, it's not a great consolation that a limited series of symbols is enough to mark the status of both the individual and the world, and that there really isn't a substantial difference, a qualitative split, between the horoscope page and the weather forecast. Start drowning in your own solitude or, if you prefer, despair, or in any other sort of interior darkness, jolly or melancholic or whatever it may be, and pretty soon you come to the certainty that deep down, the *whole world* is waiting in silence. Why it's waiting and what it's waiting for, no one knows. We didn't invite it, but it's there. Hostage of time, it gets old with us. Unable to do anything else, it desires and fails like us. One night, at the beginning of that December, I realized that it was getting way too cold in the house. Warm and gurgling as they were, all the heaters had become stolid blocks of icy metal. Our mind, our spirit, or however we wish to describe that little flame of awareness and memory that we preserve with so much jealousy, must learn to fly instead of lazily relying on the pull of gravity in order to budge. The reality is that, deprived of these minimal little wings of the soul, we are limited to *falling* into ourselves, condemned by a slip or any other unfavorable circumstance to collapse without grace into the inner well, into the sinkhole of emotions. If we could *fly down* instead, gliding delicately onto the dark lake of the heart, we could orient ourselves by way of the constellations that shine there at the bottom, maybe even purer and more luminous than the ones in the sky. On the boiler, in the lower part where the command handles reside, a red control light that I had never noticed before had gone off. This little light would shine in the middle of the night, demonstrating the boiler's surrender to inertia, its forgetfulness of itself, its neutralization of its own goals and its raison d'être that had surely been coming for weeks, if not months. The chill was growing by the minute. In every night there is a dangerous zone, some sort of blind alley where no human being, alone and pissed off, should venture frequently. Familiarity with this *night of the night*—to give it a name—discourages and destroys the identity in a very dangerous way. No environment is more hostile to the budding, healthy growth of the famous descent-assisting wings, those precious instruments that could transform us, if not into eagles, then at least into the modest but tenacious seagulls of ourselves. The warning light of the boiler would give off a weak purplish halo.

* * *

I practically recognize a Penance at first sight. In the silence of my frigid house a faint and remote lament seemed to rise, a cry for help coming from some obscure and hidden place (the bend of a pipe? the inner wall of a valve? the grid of a filter?), surely out of my reach, both mentally and manually. The boiler itself, after losing its initial self-destructive impulse, seemed regretful of the drastic consequences of its surrender to functioning. Any kind of trouble, dismay, disappointment causes in me the irresistible desire to sleep. To sleep on it. Before finding refuge under the blankets, completely dressed, I promised solemnly—not sure if to myself or to the boiler—that once up again I would find an expert, the best if necessary. The conscience of the self, *without wings*, simply falling into its black center and then resurfacing yet again more beaten and humiliated than before, scraped and scarred, grows thinner and impoverished when reduced to this predictable, worn out survival strategy. It would be very strange, if not paradoxical—I would often think during those December nights—to be able to write anything good within the gravitational pull of this system. According to my *record of malfunctions* in the hours immediately preceding the boiler's block, nothing notable had happened: at one point a sole decided to abandon the rest of the shoe, while the number of non-blown-out bulbs kept decreasing to an all time low. From the day of the seaquake to New Year's eve and then from the beginning of the new year until my departure for India, like millions of other people, I was stuck in front of the TV to watch and re-watch images of destruction. These were mostly from Thailand and Sri Lanka, where many tourists had been filming a placid and insignificant scenario of their Christmas vacations when the wave arrived: breakfast tables and hotel swimming pools, white sandy beaches rimmed with palm trees, the green-blue ocean almost dazzling in the morning sun, the ass of some passing swimmer. In selecting the material to show, news programs obviously concentrated on the dramatic moment during which the disaster burst into those meager touristy shots, devastated by the image of the wave just like, at the same moment, the real wave had devastated the tangible surrounding reality. In no case one could tell that the water, while invading those extraneous and unusual spaces, could simply limit itself to modify the field of the visible—be it the tangible landscape or a digital frame. No, the wave wasn't something that, perhaps with vehemence, had forced itself amid other aspects of the world: trees and beaches, streets and courtyards, malls, hotels, fishermen's villages, temples, cultivated fields, palm tree forests . . . In other words, its *anomaly* wasn't only because of its height, speed and all its other destructive characteristics, but also because of its total freedom from limitations, constrictions, the totalitarian dictatorship that any object in the world, big or small, endures because of its shape, because of its destiny from simply having a shape, lest it shall not exist. Liberated from this limitation, it appeared that the wave didn't have the least longing of it. If anything, its impetuosity and potency seemed destined to communicate—like an unrequested and unappreciated gift—the mysterious trait of shapelessness to all that it struck. All the hundreds and hundreds of kilometers of devastated coast that one could see in the news were, in every way, assaulted portions of the world, irreparably defaced by the pure and heartless violence of what was amorphous. The particular type of hostility that this immense force, risen from the abyss, seemed to communicate might actually make you think of the action of a colossal eraser determined to attack, once and for all, the elementary conditions of visibility of the world: its colors, surfaces, corners, perspectives, its alternating surfeits and voids.

* * *

I would sleep completely dressed; often I wouldn't even take off my scarf and shoes. I would watch TV with my coat on. I wouldn't miss a single opportunity to leave the house to get into a warmer environment. I would painstakingly attend exhibits of contemporary artists, birthday parties, book presentations, theatrical plays, work-related dinners. In other words, all the opportunities offered by a big city to connect with other human beings and enrich the spirit, but considered and appreciated by me from an exclusively *thermic* point of view. If comforted by a nice, warm place, I would've gladly partaken in a funeral wake. If, by chance, I would meet a girl while trying to hide my suspicious anxiety, I would ask her as much as I could about her heating system. Independent? Centralized? Any malfunctions at this time of the year? The rain would deconstruct the Christmas decorations into a myriad of yellowish and bluish prisms, fragments of the well-being of other worlds spreading out through the night. The parade of experts to the bedside of my boiler would carry on uninterrupted. They would ask for a ladder, and then they would start fumbling around with a perplexed air, shaking their heads and avoiding (at least that's what it seemed to me) my worried gaze. The boiler was *new*, they wouldn't miss ascertaining, and furthermore it *was working perfectly*, this statement being clearly paradoxical, and yet, in a way, indisputable. It was true: once powered up and set, the boiler would start snoring like a castrated big cat, spreading an initial veil of warmth around the house. But after twenty minutes or so, it would refuse to exist: suddenly and without explanation. The little red control light, the Star of Dejection, would resume shining weakly, while the last vibrations of the mechanism would fade and disappear in the desperate silence of the backyard of my apartment block.

* * *

There was a Coke can that was on the market in those days, one of those cans decorated with Christmas symbols, mistletoe wreaths, candles, and stuff like that. I often read what is written on cans, packages, tubes, labels. I contemplate the ingredients. Ever since I was a child, I've tried to imagine what polyphosphates and natural seasonings are, what they look like. I've studied the delicate balance of mineral water: potassium and nitrate, magnesium and chloride. On this Christmas Coke can there was a little creature dressed in rustic clothes and a pointed hat, hugging tightly, cheek to cheek, a bear cub. Under the image there was a box, sort of a scroll, with these words on it. Words whose meaning, during those endless rainy nights, I couldn't fully understand.

Nel magico mondo dei folletti
c'è posto anche per gli orsetti[1].

Translators' Note:

1. *In the magical world of sprites/There is also room for bear cubs.*

Like an orphic lamella, like a provision from an Egyptian Book of the Dead, the sentence on the can, even if unintelligible, in fact *because* unintelligible, had a certain intimidating power over me. Those words seemed soaked with an ancient and nameless wisdom, a shamanic and therapeutic power of which I was unable to take advantage. As opposed to that bear cub, which, as everyone could see, had made it, had wisely followed the instructions, had not taken the wrong path, had not missed the target. Maybe it happened to him when he least expected it and he had already lost most of his hope: there he was in the marvelous sprites' world, probably without even noticing that he had already crossed the border, now welcomed with kisses and hugs, celebrated, *loved* as if he had always been there, together with the sprites, deserving all the love that now was being poured on him. Can one be envious of a bear cub? Never in the history of humanity and of Christmas—I would reprimand myself—had such petty feelings been inspired by a Coke can. Don't get mad at the bear cub, don't envy him, don't feel cheated by his happiness, I would tell myself while trying to fall asleep under a mountain of blankets and coats: look for your own path, or get lost even more, even better. During my last glimmer of consciousness, the sprites' world appeared so far away that, in order for me to cover that distance, I would have needed the power to *elongate my life from the inside*, like you do with a fishing rod. This thought, already smeared with the tar of sleep, was the last I had. ■

Translated by Michela Martini and Elizabeth McKenzie

Francesco Verso, born in Bologna in 1973, is an Italian storyteller. He has been a full-time writer since 2009. Awards for his work include the Urania Mondadori Award for *e-Doll* in 2009, the Odyssey Award from Delos Books for *Livid* in 2013, and the Italia Award for Best Italian Science Fiction Novel for *Livid* in 2014. He was a finalist for the 2004 Urania Mondadori Award with *Antidoti umani* and received a special recommendation from the Robot Award for *Il livello dell'assassino* in 2013. His story "Two Worlds" was published in *International Speculative Fiction #5*, and his novel *Livid* was published by Xoum (2014).

The following short story was originally published with the title "*Formattazioni Celesti*" in VV AA., *I Sogni di Cartesio*, edited by Giuseppe Panella and Luca Ortino, Edizioni della Vigna, 2013.

CELESTIAL FORMATTING

Francesco Verso

An hour earlier

Marina (later called M)—So, it's set for today, then . . .

Marina's body flows on a soft wave. The water streams over her, and she absorbs it. Next to her, there's a man lying on his stomach.

Timo (later called T)—Yes, it's today.

M—What a shame, I was enjoying this configuration.

The woman glances towards the rocks to her left.

The mountain slopes sharply down to the sea. Some figures, like outlines cut against the opaque sunlight, throw themselves into the void, before re-emerging from the waves.

Marina takes off her T-shirt and floats free from a liquid which emits prismatic effects.

With a twirl, she approaches Timo's angular face as he lies on the seashore.

T—Time is not a variable which can be considered in our situation.

The drinks kiosk, a metal cube with lots of stringy spokes that cans, bottles, and snacks are hanging from, looks like a sleepy spider. All around, crowds of seagulls stomp in search of food. Further up, immense albatrosses swoop in the sky like talking clouds.

Marina starts digging an ambiguous palm-deep trough around Timo with her hands.

M—I know, but I like *fluxing* with you. In three *animations*, we haven't done it that often.

Tactile sensation is something she can't get used to. Just like grains of sand slipping through her hands.

Far away music can be heard, from beyond the dunes and the Mediterranean maquis shrubs, imbibing their ears with exotic rhythms:

After the rain comes sun,
after the sun comes rain again.[1]

Memories, whether fresh or indelible seem to be worth less to her with the passing of time. Sometimes, she even fears that they may dry up like the leaves of a perpetual autumn.

Timo wraps his legs around his girlfriend.

T—Do you want to regain lost time?

She lets him take hold of her hair, and that could be a reply to the question in itself.

M—Tell me the truth; did you ever think it could last?

T—Every time.

Surprised and full of disbelief, Marina looks at him askew.

Timo pulls himself up on his elbows. His girlfriend's hair covers his chest down to his belly.

M—And all that interference? The connection was never that stable between us.

In his steady gaze shine the sparks of a sea chopped with waves of a perfect length and cadence, so harmonic as to be almost hypnotic.

Timo continues to observe the clear, compact, slate-like horizon. He's waiting for something to happen any second.

T—Interference is part of our *relationship*. The thread can bend, but it won't break.

M—Sometimes I envy your trust. You manage to spread it over everything.

Their fingers twist over their shiny bodies. And when they brush over their skin, they emit brief sparks and voltaic arcs of pleasure.

The same thing is happening all over the beach, even if the thousands of conjunction discharges are not due to the conductivity of the water.

T—That's why you chose me from all those who were plaguing you with contact requests and *flux* proposals . . .

Although he's usually harsh and tough, in this case he gives her a smile.

Like a puzzle fitting together, Marina's mouth matches Timo's.

M—You know how to take me by the brain. Right from the first day, at the Fiuggi site, at that wonderful spa.

T—We were lucky . . . The same destination, compatible preferences, and similar profiles. The difficult part came afterwards.

---

1. From "Underwater love" by Smoke City.

Their palms unite in a pair of hands. If it weren't for Marina's ivory-colored nail varnish, they could belong to the same person.

M—But then you make me angry, when you reduce everything to pure statistical facts! We are not only the result of an event which went well. We made our choices.

T – Sorry . . . But you know I could be right. The way we met wasn't exactly romantic. I came from the Istanbul site, and you . . . you were so impatient to start experimenting. You risked connecting with a stranger. We wanted the same thing, at the same time, and we needed someone to help us forget someone else.

From her wind-tousled hair, Marina extracts a scentless magnolia. The pink-streaked flower fluctuates on the watery liquid before reaching Timo's open fingers.

M—Still, you have made some romantic gestures, even in here.

T—I hate missing the details of my animations.

In Timo's hand, the petals of the flower change color, becoming ultramarine, and just before turning towards Marina, they become adorned with arabesques and inlays, special effects that Timo learned to model during his stay at Circeo Paradise.

M—I'll never forget you. Thanks to you, I've managed to live without going mad.

A dense mist comes up from over the horizon.

Timo breathes in without his nostrils sniffing anything different than the rarefaction of the air.

T—I got here before you. You would have managed, even without my help.

The parameters around them are reconfiguring as they speak.

The curves which mark out the boundaries between their bodies and the other sunbathers break into numerous segments.

All the colors fade into a lead-coloured blotched carpet.

M – Is it starting? Is this how it always starts?

The sun, instead of illuminating the scene, reverses a dark mantle over the area. The session dissolves into a mélange of shapes.

That's when Timo yells out.

T—Save yourself. I'll do the same!

Thirty minutes earlier

A damp mist loaded with electrons slowly lifts towards a crimson sky. On Circeo Paradise beach a few pairs of bodies remain, stretched out and wet with a chrome-filled liquid.

The gulls have disappeared from the beach. On the other hand, the albatrosses dissipating above the clouds let out faraway screams.

M—Timo, I'm afraid. I thought I could make it, but it's all so absurd. Can we move?

Both of them scrutinise the jagged waves in the distance.

T—Being nervous the first time is normal and no, we can't move, it wouldn't make sense. It'll happen, anyway . .

M—How can you stand it, not knowing *when* it'll happen?

Timo's pupils dilate to take in as much of Marina as possible. He wants to brand her on his memory at maximum resolution. It would be useful later, as they advised him to do, in a public forum on their condition.

T—I just force myself to remember. It's the best way of holding on to you, and to me . . .

She reaches out a hand and pulls a drink off the mechanical arm of the kiosk, which Timo catches in midair. This gesture makes the beetle hanging from his collar sparkle, which triggers a resentful reaction in Marina.

M—You're mistaken, in Egypt you almost forgot about me. Memories that are too perfect make us lose our sense of direction. I waited a week for you to get back in touch with me . . . And I couldn't have withstood it if you had found refuge in *another site*, as you call it.

With his other hand, Timo caresses Marina's hips.

This contact doesn't generate heat, and yet, it deceives perfectly.

It's been a long time since they possessed physical sensations. And they've even stopped asking where their memories really come from. They need a surrogate, a highly-sophisticated interface, to ease the structural limits set by the animation they've transferred into.

The billowy motion drives the water level until it laps against the lovers' chests. From behind the dunes of Circeo Paradise, the melancholic notes of Portishead sound.

Wandering stars, for whom it is reserved
The blackness of darkness forever.[2]

On the foreshore, every now and then scattered sparks light up, only visible from a distance. Then, a vaporous mist descends on all of them, just before that configuration is saved and is dissolved into nothing.

Five minutes earlier

T—You have to force yourself. Concentrate and you'll be alright . . .

Marina's wide open eyes are fixed on the line which separates her

2. From "Wandering Stars" by Portishead.

stomach from her hips.

M—I can't. Just think of afterwards. Look, a piece of me . . . has already disappeared!

A wavy shape is moving around under the skin of the water like a hacked off eel's tail.

The deformation of Marina's body, like Timo's, is not due to refraction. There's something, in Circeo Paradise, operating at a lower level than perception. Something which is remixing their essences that they can't oppose.

T—Everything will be okay. In truth, *formatting* is only a temporary transfer of data. We'll find each other again.

Marina's breathing becomes shallower. She can't see her legs, and only her head's left to imagine what's down there.

M—What? Who will we be afterwards? And where will we turn up?

T—That's why you have to remember. That's the only way we'll be able to recognise each other in the midst of the channels. Please, Marina, your memory will unite us. Save the configuration . . .

M—I'm trying! But where do all the memories go if the formatting wipes away everything?

T—I don't know, but some traces remain. It's as if an echo of us manages to survive. Maybe it reverberates in a buffer soul, maybe it's reflected into a plug area where the transmigration process loses data.

Everything at Circeo Paradise is now still and even the sparks have stopped crackling: the water level does not allow for further distractions.

M—I'm having trouble believing that you can exist after so many washes.

Marina's hands lift up and an ever-thicker liquid comes out of them. A lumpy substance which sticks to her fingers and drips off slowly. The outline of her hands seems blurred.

T—I'm telling you it's like that. We have a contract and *we must* be maintained in a space of existence . . . All the spaces of this artificial hope are for giving us a possibility . . . the possibility of being rediscovered one day, by one another.

M—That's nice, Timo, but it's very abstract and I'm afraid . . . afraid that something will go wrong and puff . . . goodbye forever.

T—Listen to me, you have to remember every nuance, everything and every effect, only then can we live at a deeper level. That's why you have to engrave each other in our memories. I'll do the same.

M—Live at a deeper level? What are you talking about? Can't you see? We're disappearing! We're dying once again . . .

The air is filled with a tune Marina knows well. It's the start of "Scary World Theory," the song that Timo always loves listening to after they've *fluxed.* Only now, instead of reassuring her, it sounds harrowing.

I've never said you'll have to be afraid
of the cookie monster beside your bed.[3]

Marina starts to cry and as she does so, she squeezes her eyelids shut so that her memory of that moment will be stored in the greatest detail, so that it can last beyond the present, wherever it is deposited.

One minute earlier

Marina's tense and lengthened neck makes her spit words into the air.

M—I don't want to close my eyes and discover that you're no longer here.

The water, that has become a turbid mass, washes against their ears. When it slides into their ear canals, it feels as though their ear drums are frying: it's only one of the canals that they're about to be expelled from.

Timo tries to turn round, but the liquid laps against his nostrils.

T—When you will open your eyes again . . . my presence will be so diffuse that you won't be able to ignore me or pretend that it hasn't happened.

M—Timo, I'm afraid! I've been afraid for so long that it seems normal. I can't stand it anymore . . . At this point, it's become how I react, how I think, how I breathe. My face is itching, and I need to scratch, but I haven't got any hands!

T—Don't think about it . . . Fear often interrupts love, but sometimes love interrupts fear.

Grey droplets fall from the monotone cloak of the sky, corpuscles as light as ash. The first spots are forming on their faces, followed by deeper holes.

M—Timo, I love you, but I'm still afraid.

T—Save everything, Marina. Keeping saving, it's the only salvation.

Thirty seconds earlier

Circeo Paradise doesn't exist anymore. The level of chrome-filled liquid has become so high that the beach and all the dunes have been submerged. The condensed mist is the same color as the water. The

---

3. From "Scary World Theory" by Lali Puna.

landscape reflects a wave motion cleared of human figures.

T—Can you remember everything?

A thought spurs Marina's sinking mind.

M—Yes, but how have you managed?

The answer reverberates backwards in Timo's head.

T—It's magic. You don't need your mouth, when you know how to manipulate certain frequencies. Let yourself slip underwater. Don't resist, you're only wasting energy. Go back to the peak where we spent our first New Year's Eve. Where we saw fireworks light up the rock in Matera.

M—Yes, we were the only ones there. That memory belongs to us, just as we belong to it.

T – Well done . . . You've got it. We are like a river of memories that unwind in space and time. The forces that create its bends, depth, and capacity are not only due to the territorial characteristics but also to the river's wishes. It might seem absurd, but trust me; I've been here twice before. At the next animation, you won't need to look for me; you'll need to look for the traces of memories of where we've been together, the events where our fluxes overlapped.

Their altered consistency has almost completely dissolved.

M—What if I can't remember the right memory? What if I find someone else, someone with memories similar to ours?

T—Stop whining and do as I say. "Green grass of tunnel"[4] . . . Think of the song, sing it, sing it, sing it inside your head.

The wafting fog on the beach merges with the sea. In the space of a few seconds, the entire landscape dissolves.

A second earlier. Evacuation of the soul.

Finding each other will not be easy and looking for a unique love-profile would take years, if not decades, before being concluded. Timo and Marina, reduced to long strings of data, are two fluxes of consciousness unknown to everyone, except themselves.

Everything counts. Timo and Marina can't understand why, at least not yet, not till their next animation. Individual memories would not solve the problem and finding *only* themselves would lengthen the wait. The solution was hidden in the power of shared memories, in the homeostasis of dispersed yet interrelated entities. In whatever conjunction would remain of them.

---

4. From "Green Grass of Tunnel" by Múm.

One second afterwards

—How did it go?

Doctor Carigli approaches the lad pressing the keys of the holographic consol. With his callused hands, he is recalibrating the thousands of IP address values on the identity database.

—These logs can no longer be used. We need to reduce the bandwidth and the disk space on the server. We are receiving too many loading requests from Intensive Therapy and the Morgue.

He places his hand on the lad's shoulder.

—Where have the new funds got to? They've been promising them to us for months. We can't keep them on hold for too long. They need to be *redistributed.*

Some piles of disks lay beside the lad. Each column a meter high. His gaze is bleak.

—I know, but they're stuck. They still haven't decided how to manage the growth in transmigration requests.

Leftovers of numerous lunches and dinners are scattered all over the office.

—I understand, if you do notice any anomalies, let me know.

—I will, they'll be tighter, but they won't even notice.

As soon as Carigli has gone, the lad puts on a song and starts singing "Street Spirit."

All these things we'll one day swallow whole
And fade out again, and fade out again.[5] ■

Translated by Georgia Emma Gili

5. From "Street Spirit" by Radiohead.

Sciltian Gastaldi's exordium was with "A Family" in the Mondadori short story anthology *Men on Men 3* (2004). His first novel, *Angeli da un'ala soltanto* (Pequod, 2004, LRP, 2008), was prized as "Best Book 2005" by the Premio internazionale per l'imprenditoria gay—the Italian equivalent of the Lambda Award—and was a finalist for the Tondelli Literary Award in 1999 and 2006. His collection of short stories *Coppie* (LRP, 2009) was also a finalist for the Tondelli Literary Award. Gastaldi is also the author of the novel *Tutta colpa di Miguel Bosé* (Fazi, 2010), which was staged in 2014 through a collaboration with Fabio Canino. Gastaldi's newest novel, *Anelli di fumo*, was published in 2014 by Edizioni Transeuropa, and shares the name of his blog, which since 2004 has received over two million views.

His scholarly works include published peer-reviewed articles in international journals on Italian literature, cinema and history, as well as the historical volumes *Fuori i rossi da Hollywood! Il maccartismo e il cinema americano* (Lindau, 2004), and *Assalto all'informazione. Il maccartismo e il giornalismo americano* (Effepi, 2006). He also co-authored the Queer Studies pamphlet *Gay: diritti e pregiudizi. Dialogo galileiano contro i nuovi clericali* (Nutrimenti, 2005).

Gastaldi has published over five hundred articles in Italian magazines and newspapers including: *la Repubblica delle Donne, Diario della settimana, Il Corriere Canadese, Il Mucchio Selvaggio, Aut,* and *Babilonia*. He was awarded the "2001 Erich Fromm Prize" and the "2002 Mario Formenton Award" for emerging journalism. Finally, he is a blog pundit for the website of the nationwide newspaper Il Fatto Quotidiano.

The following is an excerpt from the GLBT coming-of-age novel *Angeli da un'ala soltanto,* which is still waiting to find an American or British publisher.

ONE-WINGED ANGELS

Sciltian Gastaldi

One

I had found it, that small bridge. Just in front of the castle, the ancient main gate, with its imposing marble angels on guard for its protection. I had passed by here a thousand times before, amidst the hysteria of bodies trapped in the metal cans that make up Roman traffic. Maybe I'd seen it at a glance while passing by, as a reflection in the rearview mirror scrutinized in a flash, while cursing at the nonsense going on behind my back. Here's the span, appearing in all of its simple beauty, bathed by the winter sun and the Tiber River surrounding it from below. I stop in the middle of the path and lift my gaze towards the grandeur of the *Mole Adriana* mansion, higher and higher until I reach the last, dominant angel. Legend goes that in 1527, while Rome was being ransacked by the Landsknechts, the Archangel Michael raised his sword from its sheath, terrorizing the wretched priests and common folk who remained in the city. That gesture was a curse, a divine curse that would fall upon everything and everyone because of the lewd behavior that had corrupted the city. Then the sacking was interrupted by the plague. The Archangel is majestic there up high. He takes the form of a forceful youth, eyes at once piteous and firm. As I move a few steps towards him, it feels like his gaze turns on me, a small, blurry speck on *his* bridge. I tilt my head a little to the right, and he slowly draws his sword, guides the blade upward, then right on me. I rub my eyes, the Archangel is still there, the sword hasn't moved. I turn away and lean on the bulwark. I slip my hand into my front jean pocket, then the one in back. I pull out my Gauloises package and light one up, snapping off the filter, so that nicotine daze might engender all that I had just seen.

Well, if nothing else this time I'm not letting anyone wait for me. Yeah, getting here twenty minutes early wasn't all that sensible—especially with this damn cold—but the day I figure out Rome's bus schedule, they'll make me mayor for sure. At least it's not raining today. Where was it he told me to stand? Beneath the fourth angel from the castle . . . so then one, two, three . . . and four. Yeah, but on which side? I dunno, so I'll just sit here, *jeez*, since you're always better off not turning your back to St. Peter's Dome, especially if you're on a bridge. "*VULNERASTI COR MEUM*," you have ravished my heart, says the inscription at the base of the marble angel in front of me. But what am I doing here in the middle of the afternoon on a bridge far away from home, waiting for someone I don't even know? More and more I stop to think whether the things I do make any sense. And the funny thing is I rarely find the answer; I rarely tell myself, "Yes, you're right, everything's fine." More and more I shut my eyes tight, press a hand over them, and tell myself I can brood over something else. It works; at least for a while.

I throw my typical *Invicta* backpack down at the feet of one of the statues and sit on it. It's an old, worn combat bag, red and blue, with all those sketches, scribbles, and statements, where a "Berlusconi poop!" stands out in block letters, and a smattering of other things: an eagle mascot from my favorite soccer team, various names, a peace symbol, and a yin-yang. At the top left it reads, embroidered in a girl's handwriting, "Francesco." A thin dreadlock is connected to one zipper, faded from use. The bottom is all worn out, and the hard cover of my *Smemoranda* diary from the previous year sticks out from one of the corners that has come undone, deformed and full of days' events gone by. As for the rest of the stuffing, a filthy pocket street atlas, creased and missing different pages, a booklet of poetry by Auden with the light blue Adelphi cover, a floppy disk, and a new-smelling copy of my fav mag, *Aut*, printed on fine paper.

Walkman, fake-leather jacket, red scarf, sunglasses, and a baseball cap; how many other guys around my age, dressed in these same colors and as haggard will pass by in the next twenty minutes under this fucking angel? At least not too many, I hope.

I stand up and look towards the river where the blond, foamy water clashes loudly. I'm not quite sure how to act on a first date with a stranger about whom all you know is that he's a damn good writer and just as photogenic. Who knows what he'll be like in real life? His first email left me speechless because it was so beautiful and perfect; I even thought maybe it was part of a prank. I spent a week convincing myself that whatever the case, it would be worth a reply—you can never tell, I said to myself—and besides, he sent me a photo attachment! Right now I'm talking about it like this and playing it cool, but when I found out that it included photos *in attachment*[1] I could only exclaim, "Ah, sure. *In attachment*!" Okay, so, I'll admit it, I'm not your typical soccer and computers type of guy; when someone says "surf" I still think about the beach, of the waves and the wind; though, with my new PC, I'm starting to get the hang of it. I also know how to use—excuse me, "surf"—the Internet. Me, I'm a quick learner. It's not like I didn't know what an attachment was, I just had no idea how to open it! I had to call up a nerdy friend of mine, Stefano, and ask for help. He's an IT wizard. Anyway, now that I know how to send things in attachment, I'd still never have the nerve to send a picture in the first email! Emanuele has already sent me five. Beautiful images: not the usual obscene Internet hookup shit. Pictures from the last two years; some taken on vacation with friends, others alone, a few in front of one monument or another. There's a couple I'm crazy about. The first of these was taken in Bologna, from atop the Asinelli Tower; he's standing alone on a corner, leaning against a merlon. He's got kind of a melancholic air about him, wears dark reflective sunglasses although the sun isn't out. He could even be sad.

Bologna isn't a city. It's *the* city. It's a second mother, portly and generous. Whenever I'm able to set aside some cash I go visit her, embrace her, and I reengage in my mental dialogue with Piazza Maggiore. I once spent three hours sitting under the portico of Piazza Santo Stefano. "*Bologna è una donna emiliana dallo zigomo forte*,"[2] Guccini the folksinger spoke into my ears, sheltering me from the

Translator's Notes:

1. In English in the original version.
2. Bologna is an Emilian woman with strong cheekbones.

December cold. The second photo was taken in Malta, on a school trip. He is cropped from the knee up. He's happy, there with other classmates whose names I still remember: Elisa, Ivana, and Alessandra. I've never been farther south than Naples, even though my roots are in part Calabrian. My mom had a falling out with the rest of her family before I was born so no one has ever brought me there. In the Maltese image I can better see Emanuele. He has short, chestnut brown hair and an angular, well-proportioned face. He seems like a pleasant person, yet has a peculiar air about him that's intriguing.

The Tiber continues to roar, yellow as urine, amid the surrounding traffic mess. Still no Emanuele. What if he doesn't come? What if this is all a joke? Maybe the asshole jerking me around is at home laughing it up. And here I am freezing. All I see is tourists in Bermuda shorts—God, they must come from the North Pole to be dressed like that on a day like this—herds of teens on a school trip and of course priests. Everything's calm, too much so even. I crouch down under the bridge bulwark; if he comes he'll catch sight of me just the same. If he doesn't come, he can go fuck himself. But, Christ, Emanuele, hurry! Or you'll only find Francesco's frozen remains.

Oh well, it's only five to three. Right, I'm not used to waiting for other people to show—unless some friend of mine is capable arriving later than me. But it's not my fault: they still have their mopeds, while mine was stolen last year. It was all tied up with a kryptonite chain and a steering wheel lock, both useless in the end. They cranked it, and *so long moped*! What a pain in the ass, needless to say I had no insurance.

From one of the *Lungotevere*, the riverside streets of the Tiber, a tall, thin guy, wearing sunglasses and a baseball cap comes forth. Is it he? He's still too far away for me to be sure. He's about to set foot on the bridge, takes his glasses off just to put them right back on. He heads straight and passes the entrance. I think if it's him and he decided not to come then he's really a jerk. But what if he got scared? He told me that he's never met anyone this way before. The first time I decided to meet someone through the personals on the "Mario Mieli" site, Rome's prominent LGBT association, was about three months ago. It was one of my first times on the Internet; I hadn't had a modem for more than a week. I don't remember where I found the URL, probably in *Aut*, the Mieli's monthly magazine. I logged on after dinner when there's less traffic and it's cheaper so my dad wouldn't get such a huge bill. I found dozens, no, hundreds of postings to reply to right away, and a total frenzy overtook me. I wrote to about twenty people because of their age, looks, and personality profile. It felt like a video game! But then, after just one day I started receiving the first replies in my inbox. At first

I wasn't worried about being too hasty; I responded to the first message and set up a date with a guy claiming to be twenty-six years old. The key word is claiming. We met a few days later, in the afternoon, despite his pushing for an evening rendezvous at the Coppedè Fountain of the Frogs. A quiet, safe, and beautiful place. The art deco style of that area bothers some people but not me. Unfortunately, instead of the "well-built twenty-six year old," as he had described himself, I'm presented with a thirty-something and far from my idea of "built." An old guy, in shorts. Nice guy, though. But I just didn't like him. He tried to pretend that everything was okay, that he was happy and self-confident, but he really just came off as a sad and lonely person. Then he proposed a second date. I told him that we would see each other again, and I would be the one to call him, since I didn't give him my home telephone number, and the most he could do was send me emails. Of course, I trashed his three emails and phone number as soon as I got home.

Unlike all of my "normal" peers, I don't have a cell phone, and I don't plan on getting one, although it would be convenient at times, like when I need to respond to the personals on the Mieli site! My classmates think I don't want a cell phone because my dad won't buy me one, but that's not true. I've always been partial to pen and paper, and I prefer a long, written conversation to a spoken one because there's more time to reflect on my words. Ever since I discovered email I've multiplied the amount of time I spend writing, even if it's different from the more "classic" style of writing: faster and impersonal, and, therefore, less reflective. But who cares: would you rather send a letter via snail mail or send an email and get a reply within a couple hours?

I'm not even sure what I'm looking for or if I'll be able to find it. First and foremost a guy that's the same age as me, to whom I can relate, talk to. It's not easy being a fag, especially at nineteen in this *splendid* papal city. At home no one knows, and, let me add, they never will. Maybe this is why I feel the need to have an accomplice, someone who is on my side and who will show me the way, to hear about how I'm getting along and maybe together we can find a better way to live. This is what being together means to me. I struggle to construct the idea of a couple at the moment. I've never seen myself from within it, not even for a few weeks at a time. I'm talking about my short-lived hetero flings, almost always the fruit of courtship pushed by one of my rather forward female classmates. Yeah, there were some good times, but I always felt like something was missing: you can't tell a girl you love her—as she would like to hear—when what you really want to talk about is how you feel about this or that guy, or what happened in the locker room with the soccer team the day before.

So I guess this is why I'm so nervous today. We exchanged numerous emails since he replied to my personal on the Mieli's website. He seems like the personification of what I'm looking for: he's eleven days older than me, he's a leftie, goes to a fine arts high school, and says he isn't effeminate. He somehow knew to delicately relate that he didn't mind sex either. He wrote, "I'm certainly not an ascetic, even if at the moment it's not my main goal in life." Perfect. Emanuele, Emanuele, when the fuck are you gonna get here? At this point I can't extend the five-minute excuse any longer. It's 3:02 p.m. Let's give him another five minutes, everybody gets five minutes . . . with Roman traffic, even a quarter past would be okay.

* * *

The term narcissism describes a condition that is both cultural and psychological. On the individual level it indicates a personality disorder, characterized by an exaggerated investment in self-image at the expense of the self.

Two

"Excuse me, are you Francesco?" says one of the angels on my right who has come down from his pedestal and turned human.

Oh my God, who . . . "Oh, yes, you're Emanuele, right?" "Yep . . ."

Strange how sometimes, a single little syllable accompanied by the right gesture can cause landslides in another person. All Emanuele had to do was take off his sunglasses to reveal a pair of eyes his photos didn't do justice to, since in four of the five shots, he had worn his inseparable rectangular Ray-Bans. Exceptional, not as much for the average brown iris as for their shape, eyelashes and eyebrows; they seemed to be drawn by a painter. He has slightly wavy, chestnut brown hair; he wears it short and you can tell it's freshly cut, leaving the nape of his neck exposed. Everything about him conveys tenderness, a beauty that makes it difficult not to lower your gaze if you don't want to be found out. He's got black, rounded boots, very cool—they look British, like Doc Martens. Judging from the crisscrossing folds you can tell they aren't new. A person's footwear says a lot about their personality. Annarita tells me so all the time; maybe it's because her mother has that Garbatella shoe shop. Above his British boots he wears a dark green pair of jeans, a white, long-sleeved T-shirt under a pale pink shirt with the cuffs up; on top he has a dark gray vest that really suits him well—it takes his stomach in and makes his upper torso jump out; he knows how to dress—in a way that gives him that personal it. Draped over one shoulder is a thick, padded jacket that I would happily have to warm my chilly body, and which—he will later tell me—he only uses when he rides his scooter. The shirt is buttoned down, and from the white cotton clothing a pendant dangling from a leather strap peeks out. I fixate on it. It's one of those hard stones, colored and round with a hole in the middle. You see a lot of them these days sold on the street. Funny. I was thinking of getting one, but I'm just not that into buying pendants, rings, bracelets, and odds and ends for myself because I find it nicer to receive them as gifts. Would you rather put a crappy chain around your neck that you bought yourself from some flea market, or carry close to your heart that permanent memory of someone thinking of you while out walking around the city? Now, I hope he hasn't the same point of view and that he bought the pendant of his own initiative. Altogether, the Emanuele who is standing in front of me gives me a certain feeling of *je ne sais quoi* from his way of dressing. Good taste, but very personalized. And who am I to say what's good or bad taste? I just mean he's got his own ideas about how to dress. Maybe it denotes character, who knows? I should have Annarita explain to me to what point the rest of one's outfit, shoes aside, translates personality.

"Yeah, it's true, you haven't changed at all . . . I mean, from the pictures that you sent me . . ." Good, I'm off to a good start.

"Yeah . . ."

"Anyway I saved *all five* of them on this floppy-thing here, in case you want them back . . ." What am I saying? Did he pick up on the irony? What a sharp tongue I have. He just arrived and already I'm picking on him. How to make up for my faux pas? Oh Lele, your pictures were so adorable: I was dying over them. Does that sound good? There you go, if you also know how to read my thoughts then I've told you.

"Oh, really? Thanks, but . . . if you want you can keep them, I obviously have copies saved on my computer, plus I have the originals printed out."

Well, if I wanted to look like an idiot I did a good job. And even worse, he knew how to make me notice. I'm such an ass! "Okay here you go, just as I imagined, it seemed a shame to send five photos like that, running the risk of never seeing them again . . . you know there are some people who try to take you for a ride . . ." What am I saying? Where the fuck did I put my cigarettes?

"No, no, I know what you mean . . ."

Don't tell me that you're speechless because I'm already struggling to come up with anything that doesn't make it seem like I've recently had a frontal lobotomy. I finally find my pack and light one. But I offer him one first, and he refuses with a clear, "No, thank you." He doesn't smoke? He didn't say so. Maybe he just doesn't like my brand.

"So, which way did you come from? I was looking at the *Lungotevere* there the whole time, what's it called, the *Alto*-something . . ."

"*Altoviti*, the *Lungotevere Altoviti* . . . no, I went around the long way because it takes less time with the scooter, traffic was blocked up down there; I came from over there and parked behind that lamppost because I couldn't drive on the bridge. Have you been waiting for a long time? I made it here a minute after three."

Why bother telling him that he's seven stupid minutes behind? "No, it's just that I arrived early; you know how it is, when you use Roman transit you know what time you'll leave but not when you'll arrive!"

"Yeah, that's true . . ." and muttering he gives me a smile that could get him a billion dollar credit line with no ID.

"Okay, well now, I dunno, you feel like a long walk and a short talk?" I ask him, trying to avoid interminable, silent pauses I can already see looming menacingly.

"How about a short walk and a long talk, if you don't mind, because it's okay that my scooter is tied up to the lamppost, but I'd like to keep an eye on it; you know, I just bought it and I spent everything I had . . ."

I try to speak in my most supportive tone of voice, "Oh, don't tell me, mine was scratched last year . . . how 'bout we do this: let's take your scooter to Piazza Sonnino; I have a friend who'll be at the Communist Party office all afternoon, you can leave it there and we can ask him to keep an eye on it. In those parts, if we want to just walk around, there are all kind of places, the Tiberina Island too. Are you up for it?" While I say this I hope that he doesn't notice my eyes light up at the hypothesis "you and I on a tandem scooter ride," and I swear, that idea only just came into my mind.

"Okay, let's go." He turns around and goes toward the Castle. His eyes will always be photographed in my mind, but now I can see him from behind for the first time . . . *damn Lele, you're skinny, and you must've left your ass on the saddle of the scooter* . . . hey whatever, I'm into skinny guys anyway.

Five hours and two cups of hot tea later, purchased mainly because when you have time to speak to someone for a while, you either drink something or smoke, but also because around seven we were both freezing—February really makes itself known—we said goodnight, deciding to see each other again the next day. Same time, different bridge: the one in front of the Tiberina is actually called "Garibaldi" and nothing less. A lot of hype for a bridge. I live far from here and don't make it out very often, so that I only know the name of the square where bus 56 reaches the end of the line. But I'll never forget where Lele lives: 22, Tondelli Avenue, at Portuense. Obviously in the boondocks behind the mountain from where I live, but I don't care; two bus lines connect us from one end of the line to the other and with our desire to see each other tomorrow it won't be a problem. It would've been great to happen to be in the same building or even the same class. But I attend the science high school, and our houses are twenty kilometers apart. My bus that'll have me home in less than an hour is finally taking off. It's started to rain outside—shit. Lele will get drenched.

As I close the front door behind me I enter into one of the most usual atmospheres of my apartment: the smell of cooking and the newscast in the background. I live in an average flat in the suburbs with my dad and my older sister, Laura, who took mom's place since her death. My mom was a unique woman. I don't remember much about her, always suspended between the indefiniteness of her dreams and the concreteness of the kitchen from where, fuming, she gave her time to the rest of the family. She wasn't happy with the lifestyle that, traitor to herself, she established with the passing of the years and habit. And if I say I am—or I was? When people die they take verb tenses with them, and I'll never know if all that I felt and that I still feel for my mother relates to the past or present; and in the end I resolve it masochistically: the beautiful things stay in the past, the ugly ones in the present—I was saying that if I say I was the youngest child and the silliest part in the family, you can believe it. Dad was able to impose his will without too much fuss, and in the end the career woman had to concede to the path of the good little housewife, all about kids and packing lunches. One of those stereotypes of love typical of a traditional *fin de millennium* Catholic society. But in the last few months Its Majesty the Cancer, the only king you can never disobey, ripped that aura of hypocritical family tranquility open. Even more quietly than mom, he had been working for years without giving any signs of existence. It had worked within her by-chance-housewife cells, having fun multiplying without criteria, making the numbers increase, the dimensions, and demands, and transporting his macabre pastime from the liver to the pancreas, from the spleen to the stomach, from the kidney to the chest. He had used and infested her lymph, spreading in metastasis to every glandular pit in that perfumed body that just a few years ago had originated the idea of me. She left in a few months. Suffering every tear of sweat that the pain of what she described as "continuous, internal lacerations" offered. Then, when the doctors put her under progressively increasing doses of morphine, her suffering partly diminished. At the expense of the last flash of life that those jealous blue eyes obstinately grabbed when Laura or I entered in her visual field.

I was eight years old at the funeral.

Still too dense to truly understand what that last, prolonged stretched out hand that she wanted to give me meant two days before, laid out by now for weeks in that king-size mattress so big for her alone. Dad, in those last days, had put a cot beside the matrimonial bed, in order not to wake her from those few moments of natural sleep when the effects of the painkillers didn't hold her in their grip. A white coffin, the kind that you use for babies and ceremonies in city hall: Mom had always been an incurable anticlerical. She, who had been a part of the 1968 Youth Revolution, a fact that she had proudly repeated to me ever since I was a baby. And I couldn't understand her. I watched her amazed, this wonder-mom, unique inventor of such a high number. A dreamer of "collective dreams," as she once responded to my obvious question about what this "68" was . . . and I used to ask my playmates to sleep together all tightly packed so that we could do the "*famous* 68" too! How I made her laugh in that moment.

When she wasn't complaining because of her eternal pain, we would play together. The thing I really loved to do in those early years was climb on her back and play horse and cowboy! A white coffin, on a morning with so much sun reflecting on its zinc cover with no cross; her last dress, custom-made, chosen—for the last time—together with a husband who hadn't been shopping with her in years. I skipped school that day, because mom "had gone." But how could she have gone anywhere in her state, I thought. And then where, with whom, since we're all at home. Then I noticed my dad's tone of voice and his strange face, vulnerable for the first time. And I understood that wherever she had gone she wouldn't be returning, at least not for a long time. Not knowing what else to say, do, or think, I cried in silence. I was afraid. Afraid the blame for that situation could fall upon me because of all the times I had made her screech or refused to obey. It's strange how you take death when you're young. With the blissful lack of awareness of one who doesn't have the faintest idea of what it means to die and above all, to survive the death of someone you love like I did; as a child, I loved my mother. Eyes full of tears, but also curious to visit for the first time that famous *Campidoglio* I had only seen on TV up until now. Rome's Renaissance City Hall was the royal palace of my fantastic city, made of the Colosseum, some ancient ruins, the Olympic Stadium, the Spanish Steps, Villa Ada Park, the Bartolomei Primary School, and the hilly gardens of Villa Chigi. Excited about the idea of entering it, to see it from within, a new Pinocchio in the belly of the whale. I remember my first thought ran to my mother: if only she could be here now!—I told myself—without realizing that she was already there: laid out in her beautiful, white coffin.

Ten years have passed since that strange morning. And even today, when I happen to pass in front of the piazza designed by Michelangelo, I feel a shudder of sadness. She left through that door. But she will never be there to reopen it.

After a few years, dad tried to find another wife without any luck. So he resolved the matter with a Filipino nanny who took care of us some and would keep the house in order when dad returned from work. Most of the time she was on the phone making international calls when dad was out. But alas, she also, after the umpteenth huge bill, left the house and my sister and my father raised me in intervals. He's a lawyer with a large firm of brainiacs from Milan, his adopted city, and I wouldn't describe him as an easy person. We have a strange and tough relationship. When I was a child we got along, I would say, even though I remember feeling a great fear every time he entered my bedroom. He was always the disciplinarian in the house, many times he didn't mind using tough measures, what he referred to as "forced education": big slaps and loud screams, to "make you understand" you had caused some trouble. Rather, pardon, you had *committed a crime* for which a *sanction* had been imposed from a *family code*, unwritten because it was based on the family traditions, which were in turn simply based on the whipping itself. Fortunately, he's convinced that the law is the mirror of the times, so he has decided to update the sanctioning system from grandpa's thrashing to the more Amnesty International open-handed smack. In any case, I am the one with the least to complain about. Listening to Laura's stories, it was up to her to open the virgin forest of paternal education by force of quick reprimands, answers, fights, armistice, and more or less bilateral peace accords. The Family. An institution of the Brusa household, competing with the mafia clans of the Coppola movies. I was raised in an almost family cult, by its rules, its schedules, its hierarchies and above all, the disappearance of mom. Laura was "promoted" from that moment on. And I was the lowest— obviously, like always. My father, reinforcing his specialization in Family Law, inherited these sacred concepts on the role and importance of family from his country-Venetian origins, when his parents would show their love not with the words that he always felt had little importance, but with actions—the *only ones* that count, as he repeats to us—along with the story about his working in the Luxembourg mines to pay for school. Mom explained my father's attitude as the result of the lack of any nuclear family ever since his earliest years. And she was Mediterranean if you know what I mean.

I love my sister, even though I feel that I lack that sense of shelter and safety at home that I would feel if I weren't gay. Unfortunately this is a big deal. I don't know how to solve my problem. Let's be absolutely clear: my being a homo isn't an issue. The problem is other people and especially, my dad. He would like me to take up his own career, a law degree, party support, loyalty to the underlying currents of the Conservative Party (the marsh of marshes, in other words) a life full of unction, minor blackmails, give and take, loyalty to whom whoever it's convenient to give it, permanent hypocrisy, routinely empty smiles, three Masses per week at rush hour so as to be seen by the electorate, some Monsignor over for dinner every once in a while, and crucifixes everywhere, even in the bathroom. All these expectations of his, so wrongly addressed, have alienated him from me. He knows how I feel about politics, he knows that I lean towards anti-clericalism, but we don't talk about it often, as intolerance is always in ambush. And then, ever since mom died I haven't felt like adding my burden to his. So, I decided I would hold my tongue forever and live my second life, far from his eyes and his brain. And it's also for that reason, ever since, that every time I enter my apartment, that feeling of shelter that my friends feel when they cross the threshold of their homes transforms into a feeling of suffocation in me, of camouflage, of inevitable strife. Just like now. ■

Translated by Silvana Mastrolia and Sciltian Gastaldi

LECCINO

Rudi Dundas

Mara Cini lives in Sasso Marconi outside Bologna, Italy. A visual artist and writer, she has published four collections of poetry—*Scritture* (1979), *La direzione della sosta* (1982), *Anni e altri riti* (1987), and *Dentro e fuori casa* (1995)—and co-authored a book of short prose entitled *Specchio convesso* (2005) with Rita Degli Esposti. Her recent poetry and short stories have appeared in numerous anthologies and magazines. She is also the editor of "*Anterem*," an Italian journal of experimental art and literature. Of the poems included here, Cini writes, "These *four scattered poems* unfold vertically, along the trajectory taken by someone studying anatomy, or a librarian intent on cataloging miniscule scenes, on carving out details from the world, without claiming to salvage only the best parts. In this forest, silent by nature and now struck by the beam of the gaze, even life shines through, life itself played out on the threshold, 'on two fronts,' that is, the *inside* and the *outside*, inside and outside history, inside and outside the possibility of closing down the old, of re-establishing the *now*."

The following series of poems, *Quattro poesie sparse*, was originally published in *blanc de ta nuque* (blog), January 3, 2007, http://golfedombre.blogspot.com/2007/01/mara-cini-inediti.html

[THE SONG SHAWL]

Mara Cini

the song shawl
a story that has only a beginning

closes in the wound
and ends there

eyelashes adorn
a verse of sleep

in the air of memory
silence comes first

unknown and unveiled
by the exodus,
by the bow

fable of the ravens
black verbs in the sky

mask of mountain
farewell of willows
greetings of sea grass

shells of the pilgrim's scallop
and witch's-claw mussels

desire to remain here
without saying

we are not leaving
always about to

time after time, the lover
is cocooned and maybe even knows it

if it is ash it once was velvet
(skin of the wrist beneath your watch)

agitation held at bay
volatile, lunatic

where you want to rest you don't rest
stubborn, I still send you thoughts

Translated by Olivia E. Sears

[GALA OF ICE, SEE]

Mara Cini

gala of ice, see
what is left

you might say ink
you might say ashes

cut and snip
whatever you want

make, cut, pull
threads and yarn both

there is nothing to say
and there is no not saying

as in *Texts for Nothing* where it says
"I say to the head"

the steps arrive
without contact, without betrayal

the steps
together with both

Translated by Olivia E. Sears

[THE GLARE OF THE NAME]

Mara Cini

the glare of the name
deflowers the entrance

a cane at the door
blocks the way

(remember the nape, the wrist
and its secret)

on two fronts
armistice is reached
running between one and the other
without fixed address

not a rock thrown
crushed stone
now this

Translated by Olivia E. Sears

[HE BRINGS THE DAY]

Mara Cini

he brings the day
in the palm of his hand:
winter's shortest day

a bunch of irises
twists into an ideogram,
withered, in december

the outside breathes silence
then the scream of a crow
then the hum of the highway
and even the whistle of a train

outside you find antlers lost
by a young deer, electrical wires,
blossoms out of season,
doormat scratched up by Léon the cat

Translated by Olivia E. Sears

Patrizia Cavalli was born in 1947 in Todi, Umbria, and now resides in Rome. She holds a degree in philosophy from the University of Rome, and an advanced degree in the arts. Her first three collections, beginning with *Le mie poesie non cambieranno il mondo* (1974), are gathered together in *Poesie* (1974–92) Einaudi, 1992. This volume was followed by *Sempre aperto teatro* (1999), which won the prestigious Premio Letterario Viareggio-Repaci. *La Guardiana* appeared in 2005. Cavalli's 2006 volume of poetry, *Pigre divinità e pigra sorte,* received the "Premio Dessì." In 2011 Cavalli published a political *poemetto* called *La Patria*. Her latest collection of poetry, *Datura*, appeared in 2013. Finally, a selection of her poems appeared in a bilingual edition, *My Poems Won't Change the World: Selected Poems by Patrizia Cavalli* (Farrar, Straus and Giroux, 2013). Cavalli has also written plays for the Italian radio, and collaborated with several musicians. She is a well-known translator of plays by Molière and Shakespeare.

Cavalli's unique poetic style is characterized by brief, epigrammatic lyrics and a subtle musicality, and the tension between classical poetic forms and a colloquial lexicon.

"[I fall and fall again]" is from *Pigre divinità e pigra sorte*, Einaudi, 2006.

[I FALL AND FALL AGAIN]

Patrizia Cavalli

I fall and fall again, stumble and fall, I get up
and I fall again, relapses are
my specialty. What else have I done
but pretend to go out only to fall back in?
Never would I drag anyone down with me
as I fall. Powerful balance surrounds me
but doesn't hold me up, in fact it is because I fall
that others stand tall. How beautiful
that couple of old lovers, who arm in arm,
wanting to test themselves with a double dare
against the chain that closes off Ponte Sisto
convinced that their staying together would have
held them up, instead they fell together
still arm and arm, not embarrassed
but quite astonished that their being
paired so perfectly had unbalanced them,
yet grateful to one another
for being in two, so that neither of the two
if safe, would see the other fall.

Translated by Margaret Brose

Angela Scarparo was born in Brindisi in 1959, lives in Rome, and has written film scripts and literary and art reviews for the Italian papers *Il Foglio*, *il Manifesto*, *la Repubblica*, and *Luogo comune*. She published the novels: *Shining Valentina* (Mondadori, 1993), *Quando cresci in un piccolo paese* (Transeuropa, 1995), *Disturbando famiglie felici* (peQuod, 2005), and *Volevamo essere giganti* (Gaffi, 2012); in 1984 her poetry book, *Virtù*, was published. She wrote and produced the theatre plays *Lola Italiana* and *Ode al terremoto*. She has a law degree with a dissertation on Franco Basaglia.

The following short story was originally published with the title "*La passeggiata di Randi e Antonia*" on VV. AA., *Una bella bici che va...*, edited by Isabella Borghese, Giulio Perrone Editore, 2014.

THE WALK

Angela Scarparo

She was too tired to ride a bike, she would not have gone there. But if she took it with her. She did not want Mary, the maid, using it. It was hers.

She knew that her mother wanted her to do at least a little tour, every day.

"Fuck you, mom! To you and your bike!" she thought.

She would have said that she was there, that is what she would have done. So her mother would never have noticed.

She met Virginia who was going to study in the library. She was taking the car.

"Why do you need to take the car? Why not go with the bike?" she asked her sister.

"Because I am coming back late tonight . . . and you?"

"I ride my bike, do not you see me?"

"I see you. Great. I have to run, see you later . . ." said Virginia.

Antonia watched her go. The neighbour's dog came up to her. He kept his tail low and wagged it. She felt the need to give him a kick. The windows of Maria Sole, the owner of Randi, overlooked the courtyard. Antonia pushed the front wheel of the bicycle to the dog, who dodged, and still approached her, with lowered tail and watery eyes, the eyes of someone who loves everyone.

"Go away . . ." she said softly.

The dog, as if she had said something nice, moved closer.

As if by accident, she dropped the bike, which only touched him.

The dog backed away, but was not scared. He watched her from a short distance, his head straight, like a person who expects to be recalled.

Antonia had an idea. With a little effort, because her mother had raised the saddle, she mounted the bike.

She cursed her: "With the saddle so low, it is no use to you!" she had said. Antonia snorted. She was not bad looking, as a girl. And maybe if she had accepted that she was not the number one girl in the world, the most beautiful, the most intelligent, perhaps she would be less unhappy.

She spent her time overseeing the kitchen, and stealing pieces of cake, or tins of food, bags of salmon, containers of stuff that her mother or Mary, the Filipina maid, put in to freeze. The mother only yelled at her when she could not stand it any more. And then she said bad things: "You're insufferable, Antonia! Why do you not wait till lunch time? Stop avoiding us! But how can you not understand that you're ruining your life?"

But usually, because she believed herself to be an expert in anthropology, she was silent.

Antonia was convinced that, every time she stole something and devoured it behind a bush (in the bathroom, or behind the car, down the road, or, if the house was empty, in front of Mary) in the end, she was re-establishing some form of justice.

She was the most intelligent, she was the most beautiful . . . well, perhaps not beautiful, Virginia was prettier than her, but then, she was right, however, in wanting to re-establish some form of justice: "Oh, God, why did you not arrange that I was born the best?" she pleaded. "It would have been enough to put in a little more of dad's cells, and less from that moron my mother. Then, instead of this bitch of a bike with this turd of a dog, which I will drive away in a few moments, I'd be in some hotel, located in a beautiful bath, with the music of the Draft Punk, and the best chocolates in the world in my hands!"

The dog was following her. They had embarked on the cycle path leading to the pool. She pedalled gently. The mother had told her to get to the sports center. "If every day you do a couple of miles, eventually you'll feel better!" she had shouted to her from the bedroom. She would have wanted to add, "And you'll even be less crazy!" But she did not.

"Why should I . . ." replied Antonia. And she, like her mother, had not said the second part of the sentence, ". . . feel better!" she thought.

The dog was walking in front of her now.

She stopped the bike. She got out of the saddle. Her feet firmly on the ground.

"The dog trots . . ." she thought. Resting on the handlebars of the bike, she looked at him. There was a harmony in the way he moved his feet: the two in front, moving in perfect agreement with those behind.

It was fun. They made no noise, but it was as if they did.

"*Tlo tloc . . . tlo tloc . . .*" thought Antonia.

She turned back to look at the houses. There was nobody. Basically she was walking Maria Sole's dog for her, she thought, and it was not fair.

"Randi, come here!" she said. "Go back." She put the bike sideways now.

"Go home, go on!" she repeated.

The dog stopped, looked at her, he made a motion with his head, as if to say, "Come on, let's go!" and proceeded.

"But why do I have to go around with your fucking dog, oh, Maria Sole!" she said aloud then. "At this moment you'll be reading, or making love with your atrocious boyfriend."

The dog had gone on further. He was sniffing the grass at the edge of the road. "What then, if only I could meet him alone, and if I feel like it, my dear stupid, fucking forty-something, if I wanted to, I could also pinch your boyfriend off you! Nasty old bitch! Randi, come here."

The dog had now gone into the field.

Although there was high grass, he could still run into the middle. "Randi!" The dog continued to run in the tall grass.

Antonia got back on the bike, began pedalling. Slowly, at first, then faster. There were no cars on that road, and at least she could avoid the fear of ending under a truck.

She pedalled strongly now, confidently, she felt hot, she wanted to get to the sports center without stopping. Once arrived there she would eat a cold *focaccia*, and would take a Coke. She deserved it. And even a chocolate bar. She would not pay, she would sign for it on her father's account, as he had told her explicitly not to leave debts around. Given that she thought his life was elsewhere, and he definitely preferred to stay with his woman, instead with her and her mother, he could at least pay for her snack. She pedalled and pealed, trying not to think about Randi.

She knew that Maria Sole did not want the dog to come out of the yard. He had already been lost twice. The first time he had followed Anita, the other neighbor, the second time her mother, and both times someone had phoned to say come and collect him. But it was the cars that Maria Sole was afraid of.

"Why does she not keep it under control, it's her dog?" thought Antonia. She stopped the bike again. She got out of the saddle. She turned around. The dog was running towards her, in the middle of the road. With his flying ears drawing a kind of halo all around his head, and his mouth open, as if he was smiling, he was coming to meet her like a person arriving late at the station. He ran almost as if he wanted to make up for lost time, to stay together.

He caught up with her.

"Hey," smiled Antonia. "Come here." The dog began to greet her excitedly. He jumped up on her knees. She gestured with her hand on her thigh. "Here," she said. He put his paws on her arm. He licked her, an act that was tantamount to a kiss.

"No! Stay down! Enough is enough. Stay down!" she said. The dog put his legs down on the ground again. Then he sniffed the asphalt. He walked a few feet. Again he slipped into the field, but on the opposite side of the road, this time, where the grass was much higher.

Antonia was afraid that he might get hurt. She felt very hot. With the bike leaning behind her back, she stared at the field, and began to think about what would happen if a snake had bitten Randi. Her mother always told her when she was little, "Do not go out alone! It's dangerous."

She called him. "Randi! Come here." The dog must have crouched, because she could not see him any more. Then she stood up a little on her toes. She raised her head.

The grass was too high.

"But why does the summer have to come, at some point," she thought.

And, "What a bore!" she shouted.

"Come!" This time she screamed. Again on tiptoe. She did not see him, but she could imagine that he was there, down. She gently let down the bike to rest on the ground on one side.

She reached the edge of the road, as Randi had done before. She was afraid to enter in the midst of the weeds. She had cloth dancing shoes that did not protect her feet.

"Randi!" She called. Then she saw the grass become agitated, as if a strong wind was moving it from within. And she saw the dog's back, mottled brown and white.

She clapped a hand on her thigh. The white dress with blue and sky blue flowers stuck to her back when she made that gesture.

Randi came out of the tall grass with a little effort.

He had a little clump of vegetables in his mouth, or something that looked like that. Antonia bent down on one knee, her leg naked in front of the muzzle of the dog who placed his gift to Antonia on the ground: a rat.

It must have been dead for a while, because its head had been completely crushed on one side. You could see the teeth very well. The girl stepped back and her left foot struck the bicycle wheel, which began to turn. Randi bent down on his front legs, began to turn. Randi bent down on his front legs, leaving his rear legs immobile. It was his way of saying he wanted to play. Antonia knew that. The bicycle wheel continued to spin. ■

Translated by the author

LOVE-IN-A-MIST

Rudi Dundas

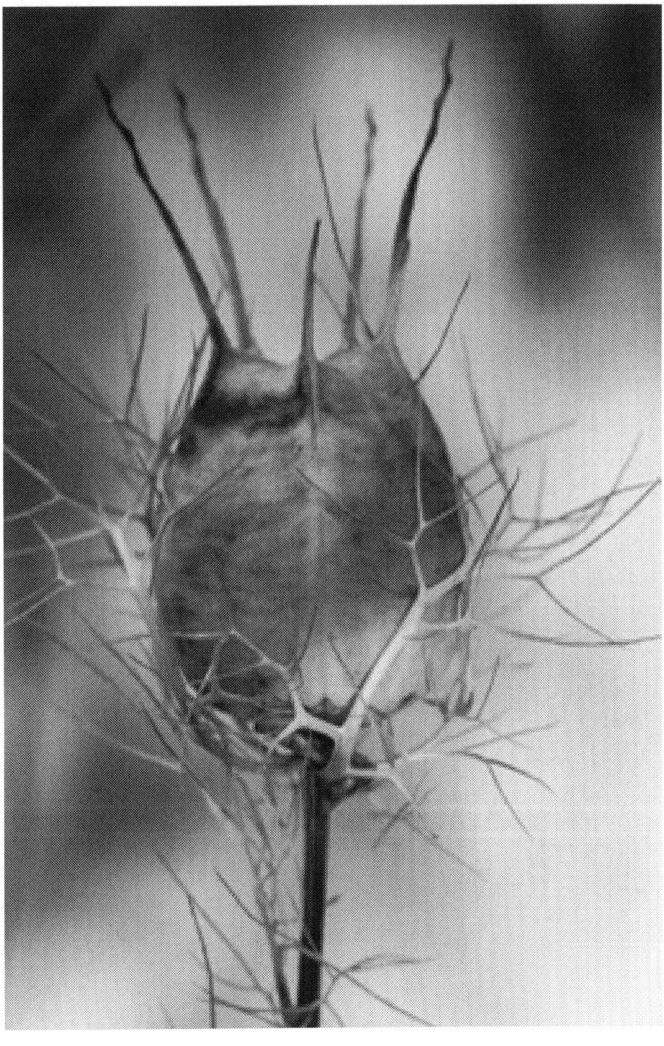

Massimo Migliorati was born in Brescia, Italy, where he lives and teaches. In 2011 he received a doctorate at the Università Cattolica of Milan for his work on Ungaretti's critical studies. Migliorati's writings on the poetry of Giuseppe Ungaretti, Giovanni Giudici, Carlo Porta, and Luciano Erba appeared in the journals *Testo*, *Letteratura e dialetti*, and *Otto/Novecento*. He was also the editor of the texts and translations (from the Milanese dialect) of Carlo Porta's *Poesie* (Oscar Mondadori, 2011). His published work includes the plaquette *D'intorno* (Campanotto, 2006, with an afterword by Alessandra Giappi), and the collections *Qualcosa del resto* (Campanotto, 2012, afterword by Giancarlo Pontiggia) and *Città* (Campanotto, 2014). Uncollected poems have appeared in the journal *Città e dintorni* with a commentary by Franca Grisoni.

The following poems are unpublished.

[ONLY THE SURPRISE OF BELLS TOLLING]

Massimo Migliorati

Only the surprise of bells tolling
sets time free, gives back the look,
puts back in the heart what has been,
and lets the changed wind speak.

Translated by Patrizia Villani

[WHO KNOWS IF THE WIND INTRIGUING US]

Massimo Migliorati

Who knows if the wind intriguing us
and ruffling our hair really loves us
or not; who knows whether it knows of us
and brushes against us in the same way as
the water of the lake or the mountain snow.

Translated by Patrizia Villani

[THEN WE RECOGNIZE OURSELVES, NOW AND THEN]

Massimo Migliorati

Then we recognize ourselves, now and then,
and weakly, in a reflected image,
it's not a spring, neither the mirror,
we see ourselves again—that's it—in the quivering
of a puddle, in the marine
rippling of the water, like a shudder
of something we don't know and yet moves us.

Translated by Patrizia Villani

[AND THEN, IF YOU THINK ABOUT IT, THE REST]

Massimo Migliorati

And then, if you think about it, the rest
vanishes into the silence
like a large womb
containing all
similar everywhere always
like a grief following
and forgetting it has us
that comes back one and only
together with recollection.

Translated by Patrizia Villani

[THE PANES STREAKED BY THE RAIN]

Massimo Migliorati

The panes streaked by the rain
follow in succession, toward the horizon
other panes streaked by the rain,
between them walls of different colors;
branches line the sky, bones
a tangled mass of fingers
pointing upwards
and further behind a pinaster, an elm
another bugbear.
Raindrops are streaking the panes
and behind, further behind
life follows in succession
and nobody knows what it is.

Translated by Patrizia Villani

[TODAY IS A DAY OF WIND]

Massimo Migliorati

Today is a day of wind,
to be spent at the window
watching the show outside,
how the rest is stirring that we are not
without torment
to look is to assist
to put oneself out and put oneself in;
to release what else is with us
not stare at one's toes
without wonder
to listen to what's moving
like the sea in the shell.

Translated by Patrizia Villani

Alessandra Lavagnino, a biologist, was an associate professor of parasitology at the University of Palermo, Italy, until her retirement and is the author of many papers on tropical disease vectors, three books of popular science, and several novels and short stories. In 1968 she was awarded a prize for an unpublished manuscript for the novel *I lucertoloni*, (Mursia, 1969), republished by Sellerio in 2005 as *Via dei serpenti*. The book was translated as *The Lizards* by William Weaver for Harper and Row (1972). *Una granita di caffè con panna*, (Mondadori, 1974 and Sellerio, 2001), is perhaps the first novel set in a mafia context seen through the eyes of a woman. It has been published in Slovak and Spanish, and in English as *Truth and Flies* (Troubador Storia, 2010). Her novel *Le bibliotecarie di Alessandria* (Sellerio, 2002) won the New York University Zerilli-Marimò Award for Italian fiction in 2002. The English translation was published by Steerforth Press (2006) under the title *The Librarians of Alexandria*. *La madre dell'ultimo profeta* (Edizioni dell'Altana, 2004) is an imaginary biography of Elizabeth, the mother of Saint John the Baptist. The opening chapters appeared in English in *Comparative Critical Studies* in 2014.

Un inverno 1943-1944 (Sellerio, 2006) records a secret operation to rescue Italy's artistic heritage during the Allied invasion. This book has inspired a television documentary and an international conference held at the Vatican in 2012. The following is an excerpt from *Un inverno 1943-1944*.

In this extract the author quotes frequently from the diary of her father, Emilio Lavagnino, which recounts his work for the team which was dedicated to rescuing the artworks of central Italy from destruction by Allied bombing.

ONE WINTER 1943-1944

Alessandra Lavagnino

February and March

Over the next few days, my father meets his colleagues from the Ministry—both retired[1] and not, both pro- and anti-Ministry—to organize the protection of the other monuments and churches of Viterbo and Santa Maria della Quercia . . . but there is no news of the money that is supposed to be coming from Padua.

He is convinced that our destiny is to come out of the war in pieces, and that "tanks will roll over the ruins of our villages"; that the Allies, with their landings in Sicily, in Calabria, at Salerno and then Anzio,

Translator's Notes:

1. The "retired" civil servants are those, like the author's father, who were dismissed for refusing to take orders from the rump Fascist regime in Padua. They carried on working regardless.

really want "to roll Italy up like a rug" while "only Rome, maybe, will be saved."

He plans new journeys in Lazio, and if possible to Umbria and Abruzzo. He writes: "We need to go from village to village along the Via Aurelia, the Cassia, the Tiberina, the Flaminia, the Salaria, the Tiburtina, and if possible the Via Casilina too—the Via Appia is out of the question now—to bring to Rome as much as possible of what is left in the churches. If they give me a permit to use my Fiat Topolino, I can do the journeys by myself." He asks Palma Bucarelli to lend him three tires from her car. She promises to do that, and her old friends the Lucarini brothers—Achille and Danilo, mechanics in Piazzale Flaminio—will find him a battery.

Scheibert[2], enchanted by the idea of a car journey to see new places and new people—especially bishops—gets my father a two-week driving permit. Palma lends him the three tires, and the Lucarinis supply the battery—from a client who "has a car hidden somewhere." The Topolino is carried by truck to Palazzo Venezia, where Getulio ties it to the back of Vannutelli's Balilla, puts it in gear and gets it going. After a few turns around the Piazza, thanks be to God, he's off . . . ! "At last, after so long, I'm driving my own car again! De Rinaldis, who is better now, is delighted by this; he hasn't said a word to anyone at the Ministry. The plan is to shoot off the day after tomorrow with Scheibert and Mercurelli down the Via Cassia as far as Acquapendente."

February 16th. "First stop, Sutri. The most important pieces here are the Salvatore in the Cathedral and the Marten de Vos in the Church of the Nuns. Scheibert, disappointed that the Bishop isn't at Sutri but at Nepi, went with Mercurelli to visit the Cathedral's crypt. Meanwhile, I talked to the Bishop's deputy, and in Scheibert's absence I was able to speak freely, making him vividly aware of the dangers from bombing, artillery, evacuations and looting. The deputy told me that he would make arrangements for keeping the church's treasures safe in dry places, ideally underground. I leave a letter for the Bishop in which I say I'll return in a week to collect the Salvatore and the Marten de Vos. Sutri worries me, being at the head of a gorge, a perfect place for an army to make a stand, but nobody there seems to share my concerns.

"At Vetralla things are very different. Since the bombings in January, Vetralla has been completely abandoned by its inhabitants. This has caused looting by both Italians and Germans, so that today the village looks as if the war has been fought through it, street by street. Nothing is left in the shops; windows have been smashed and doors

2. An SS Lieutenant on whom Emilio Lavagnino depended for travel permits and fuel.

torn off their hinges; there's not a sign of life. Not even the parish priest. I met a young monk coming up from the church of San Francesco and gave him a note for the priest, asking him to hand the Madonna from the Cathedral over to the monastery behind the town cemetery, and saying that I'll be back to collect it."

Then, at Viterbo, Lavagnino insists that the local administration should take steps to protect the frescoes by Lorenzo da Viterbo in the church of Santa Maria della Verità, and recommends the storing of all the altarpieces from the Museum and churches in a safe place within the Archbishop's palace.

Montefiascone. "The Bishop is old, but still at his post, and highly intelligent. He assures me that he has already made arrangements to hide all the most valuable items from the churches in his diocese.

"At Orvieto, walls have been built to protect the sculptures on the Cathedral façade, but nothing has been done for the Gentile da Fabriano. All we can do is pray."

Back in Rome, Lavagnino telephones his sister, who says, "Lie low. They've arrested your colleagues from the Ministry." He rings Argan, who tells him how, during the night and early morning, nearly all the officials were arrested, but not the technical staff. He goes home, up in Monteverde, and asks his lodgers to say he's out of Rome if anyone comes looking for him. Then he packs a small case to take with him to Palazzo Venezia where he'll spend the nights. The lodgers were the old Russian Jewish couple. It all worked out fine.

On February 25th another journey in the Topolino, with Major Evers and Montenovi in the car, and three trucks—this time to Sutri, Vetralla and Caprarola. They go together as far as Montenovi, where the trucks separate: two, with Giorgio Rosi and Krapf (Major Evers' Deputy) on board, go to Caprarola to load up objects from the Gallery of Modern Art, while the other one will bring back the Madonna from Vetralla Cathedral and the Marten de Vos from Sutri. Meanwhile, a lot of bombs are falling on an airfield nearby. At Ronciglione they see a German truck go by carrying the injured. The "things" in the Gallery of Modern Art are to be stored inside the spiral staircase of Castel Sant'Angelo.

February 28th. A strange lunch. My father writes: "The evening before last, Evers rang and invited me to have lunch with him today. I tried to tell him that I had to accompany Monsignor Costantini to Tivoli, and I didn't know if I'd be back or free at that time, but he insisted so courteously that I couldn't refuse, even though being seen with a German officer in uniform would annoy the hell out of me. In fact, my appointment with Monsignor Costantini isn't until tomorrow.

"And so today at 1pm precisely I was just outside the Colonna restaurant as agreed, when a familiar group appeared around the next corner—Scardamaglia, De Gregori, Rosi, Gregorietti, and Senator Bartoli.

"The situation was so comical that I couldn't help laughing. Extremely embarrassed, Scardamaglia held out his hand, and I shook it, but I told him that if I'd known the invitation was an official one, I wouldn't have accepted it. Since there was nothing to be done now, we went in together. Inside we found Evers with other German officers from the Roman HQ, a Lieutenant Colonel based in Florence, and two or three characters in civilian clothes, one of whom was Dr. Lang, the Austrian from the History Department. Then Curtius arrived.

"Evers made the introductions, and gave a little speech on the noble aims of our mission; Curtius translated and Scardamaglia responded as best he could. The real fun began when we sat down to eat.

"The places were marked with cards. I looked for mine at the corners of the table, but to my immense surprise I found it in the center, next to Evers, in the second highest place of honor among the Italians. Opposite me were Scardamaglia and the Lieutenant Colonel, and to either side the Germans and Italians were arranged pretty much at random.

"Scardamaglia had seemed to be in a thoroughly foul mood to start with, but after the wine had mellowed him a bit, he put a brave face on the situation and ended up admitting to me that personally he didn't have an opinion one way or the other about my activities, and that in any case they should stay invisible from the official point of view, because over in Padua they were highly irritated that the department for protection against bombing attacks was still operating here in Rome.

"According to Padua, the department was going to work from Castel Sant'Angelo, where (between ourselves) they would be distributing compensation, et cetera. I put his mind at rest on that point. Compensation? With what, when he knew perfectly well that no such funds existed?

"As we left the restaurant, Scardamaglia instructed Gregorietti to send an account of the lunch party to Padua, with the recommendation that no mention should be made of my name. Rosi was highly amused. A few days ago he had been appointed by Padua to take over responsibility for the artworks in the Vatican, and to manage the removal of artworks from their currrent depositories into safekeeping. In other words he is supposed to do what the Ministerial Commission, and I, have been doing up till now. Despite this, I intend to carry on with my work, and we have been able to agree on that. With respect to the items being stored in the Vatican, I certainly won't object if the clerical chores are placed in Rosi's hands."

* * *

I see that 1944 was a leap year: the diary refers to a journey made on February 29th, the journey to Tivoli with Monsignor Costantini, Chairman of the Papal Commission for Sacred Art. Tivoli has already been affected by bombing, and yet the Bishop will not hand over the Cathedral's painting of the Savior. He says that if the Savior were to be taken away, the people would rebel and he would fear for his own safety. "We send for the 'Chief Warden' of the image of the Savior, and go with him to look at a cavern near the Cathedral. We tell him that if danger threatens, he must take the Savior there for safekeeping. On our journey back to Rome Monsignor Costantini is rather downhearted at the hardly brilliant outcome of our intervention...."

March 2nd: in never-ending rain, a journey to Rieti with Major Evers in the Topolino. They organize the protection *in situ* of the Episcopal Archive and Library, and select items for taking back to Rome at the earliest opportunity. On the way back, Evers asks to be dropped at his HQ in Sette Bagni.

"Having stopped at the side of the road I notice a stampede into the countryside and into the German camp. Three large aircraft are flying nearby, very low. I can make out the three black shapes in the uncertain light of a cloudy evening. Sitting in my car, with the engine running because the battery is low, I follow their flight and see that a few kilometers away they turn right, and aim for Sette Bagni station, which is where I am. I put the car into gear to get out of there, but I've only gone a hundred meters when the great hulks pass roaring overhead. Looking up, I see crosses painted on their wings. Evers, who's popped up from goodness knows where, guesses what's on my mind and says, not without a barb of irony, 'It's lucky they were German this time'...."

* * *

I was still meeting up with my father for lunch at the convent in Borgo Santo Spirito, and sometimes he'd tell me—and Fritz Volbach, who was nearly always there—about his travels. But I didn't pass these stories on to my aunt or grandmother. My visits to their house were still pilgrimages to a childhood that I wanted to remember as happy, even though the present had contaminated them. I would stay a while, often in silence, and then leave. Sometimes, having rung the bell, I would hear someone close the door of "Norina's room," the book-filled room which had lately been my grandfather's. Then my aunt would come to let me in, greeting me as always with "Hello, kid;" but she wouldn't look me in the face and there'd be something strange about her eyes. I didn't notice at first, but she never went into that room while I was there. Later I thought that perhaps she only went in to tidy the books, and the dust got into her eyes.

Once we had gotten through that freezing January and February, the longer days made us want to start doing things, to open the windows, to be outside.

Across the courtyard, from the floor above, came the sound of a piano. Small hands. A little child. I called up from the recesses of my memory, from the time before Mamma left, pieces I had learned in the few absent-minded lessons she'd given me. Until she'd gone.

The curfew was at five, and it was still cold then, but much worse in the mornings when I went to school. I had already eaten half my roll, with a quarter-liter of milk from my grandmother's ration: that was breakfast. The rolls were dark, half-cooked and soggy, made from flour mixed with who knows what, and they smelled of mold. I found it hard to save the other half for later in the day. Two rolls would have seemed like a feast. On my way to school, wrapped in my woolen scarf, I sang The Submariners' Hymn:

In deep black night they cut the waves across the open sea,
Turrets by the thousand, spying out for prey,
Swift and never failing, submarines are sailing,
Hunters setting out to win the day,
Mighty engines, mighty hearts against the deep immensity![3]

Et cetera. The rhythm was good for coping with the cold, even if the images—the black night, the engines and the immensity—had nothing seductive about them.

* * *

[*Sixteen year-old Alessandra is shuttled between her two grandmothers' houses for safety. She is currently with her maternal grandmother. A Jewish family lives in the same block, and sometimes the neighbors can hear the sound of their little boy having piano lessons.*]

At Via Tacito my other aunt had started talking to herself. She was

3. This Fascist morale-booster, the *Inno dei Sommergibilisti*, can be heard on YouTube.

white-haired now and had given up using curlers, which seemed to me like a further piece of self-neglect until, staying in her house, I realized that she kept them in her hair at night. I was happy there in the apartment that had been my childhood home. While I was with Grandma and Auntie I could recall better days when Mamma was with us, and (thinking back on it now) time seemed to be standing still, or oscillating between past and present: a holiday from those unbelievable months.

Sometimes, Grandma would stare at me, and then look down as if she never intended to lift her head again. But I didn't ask her why. There were already too many things going unsaid between us.

I used to hear music coming from the courtyard as I translated my Homer and Cicero, and I'd imagine the little boy sitting at the piano with his feet on a little stool that covered the pedals. He was good. I said so once, pointing in the general direction of the window. My grandmother looked at me for a moment, and then turned away. Eventually she said, "It isn't him." She was silent a while longer, and then she said, "They took him away, two weeks ago, with his parents and his grandmother. The Germans, early one morning. They knew exactly where to find them. It's not him, but don't say anything to your aunt. Don't tell her you know it's not him. She knows, but keep quiet about it. It's dangerous."

So I would only look out into the central courtyard, the one with the little forest of plants, when no one was playing the piano. I knew that Augusto, the caretaker, watered the plants—but only in summer, not now. When he was out there, could he tell where the music was coming from? But that didn't occur to me straight away.

On my way to school every morning, to my class that now consisted only of girls, I called in at the apartment for books or to change my shoes, dipping back into my other life, and then I bought my roll. Papà gave me money when I met him for lunch at the convent in Borgo Santo Spirito with Volbach, who scratched his spots and made them bleed—a small, repellent fact that I can't forget and which gave me a sense of his desperate loneliness.

"It's not him," said my grandmother, and those words stayed with me like a kind of nausea. Then one day I saw a German notice with its characteristic black border on the wall next to the egg shop—which still supplied the egg ration even though it no longer had chickens, just the smell of them left in the straw. The proclamation read: "All building supervisors are required to notify the authorities of any Italian citizens of the Jewish race living in the buildings entrusted to their care: Office of the German High Command in Via Ennio Quirino Visconti, number...." (No, I don't want to write that number today. It was right next door, a few meters away.) Every caretaker in Rome would have had to report to that office, travelling either by bicycle or on a Circle Line bus, but for Augusto it had been a matter of a few meters. He only had to cross the road. He would have been shown in—promptly, efficiently—he would have produced the right documentation, or perhaps simply given a name and told them all they needed to know about the family of the little boy who played studies by Duvernoy with his feet on the stool. Did they need all the names? Maybe not—but he would have given all of them in any case. The Germans always let expelled Jewish families take their keys with them, to keep them calmly believing—and how could they not?—that they would be coming home again.

The German decree was dated February 23rd, less than a month ago. Augusto had gotten busy pretty soon after that. So who was playing Duvernoy now? Grandma had said, "It's dangerous," and naturally I didn't talk about these things with my father.

Through the kitchen window I saw that a basket was hanging from a rope next to the window of "Norina's room," from where it wound around a small hook and reached the floor above. My aunt put things in that basket: things to eat. Then someone pulled the basket up. The pianist, whoever he was. I realized that my grandmother knew. It was the little boy's teacher. Although he was Jewish too, he had stayed in the apartment. Perhaps he had even been there on the night of the abduction—"very few people were sleeping in their own beds"—and hidden while the others had been taken off because their names were on a list. The door of the apartment was double locked, and now he played his pupil's music all alone up there on the fifth floor where the caretaker couldn't hear, or didn't understand what he should be listening out for. Other people, people like my grandmother, my aunt, and me—we heard, we understood, and we kept quiet.

It was now late March and, although we couldn't know it at the time, the music would continue until June when the Americans would finally enter Rome. We had a few provisions stored in our apartment, and meanwhile the piano teacher played beginners' exercises by Pozzoli and Duvernoy—slowly, nostalgically, with the utmost care. The nostalgia is my own—and I feel it no less in thinking about him today. We were all grieving children during those months, even my grandmothers (both of them), and my teachers at school—my father too—because we were all so hungry and cold. Listening to Pozzoli, I stole an egg, wrapped it in paper and put it in the basket which was hanging just under the window sill. And whenever he wasn't playing

I thought "he's gone"—but the door was locked, could he have found another key?—or else I thought, "they've found him."

As the years have passed, I've gone over in my mind the reason why he denied himself the greats like Beethoven and Chopin; although he allowed himself a little Bach—"the consoler" as he's been called—but in simplified versions for children. The pianist reined himself in and ignored the great composers so that he could reincarnate the childish music of his abducted pupil, the little boy who would never grow up.... Yes, it's easy rhetoric, but it feels right now, sanctified by time. I know it's only words, but there are times when words are all we have left. It's different for musicians. They have another language in which they can speak or be silent, reveal or wound. They can't lie, but they can betray themselves. Did the boy's piano teacher want to betray himself? Was he defying fate? Playing a mocking game with the Nazis?—or just with Augusto? The shame—the shame of that Augusto. And his fear, of course. A vile need to obey, to be "on the right side of the law," to be seen to be "doing his job."

I put two onions in the basket. Later I smelled frying. So he had a bit of oil up there. In the days and weeks that followed I saw other baskets and bags hanging under the windows of the central courtyard, and the ropes all led to the fifth floor. Maybe some of them contained little bottles of oil. Butter was out of the question. We didn't yet have margarine: that was a great novelty after the war. Now they say it's bad for us. There was "lanital," fake wool made apparently out of milk and casein. I had two sweaters made from it: a silver one with short sleeves, and a cardigan. Lanital, casein: grand words for these home-made things. Jokes. Tiny echoes of great tragedies.

Maybe my aunt put her curlers in at night and not by day, so that the musician on the fifth floor wouldn't see her with them in her hair. I never even knew his name. ■

Translated by Adam Elgar

ONE WAY

Rosebud Rosabella

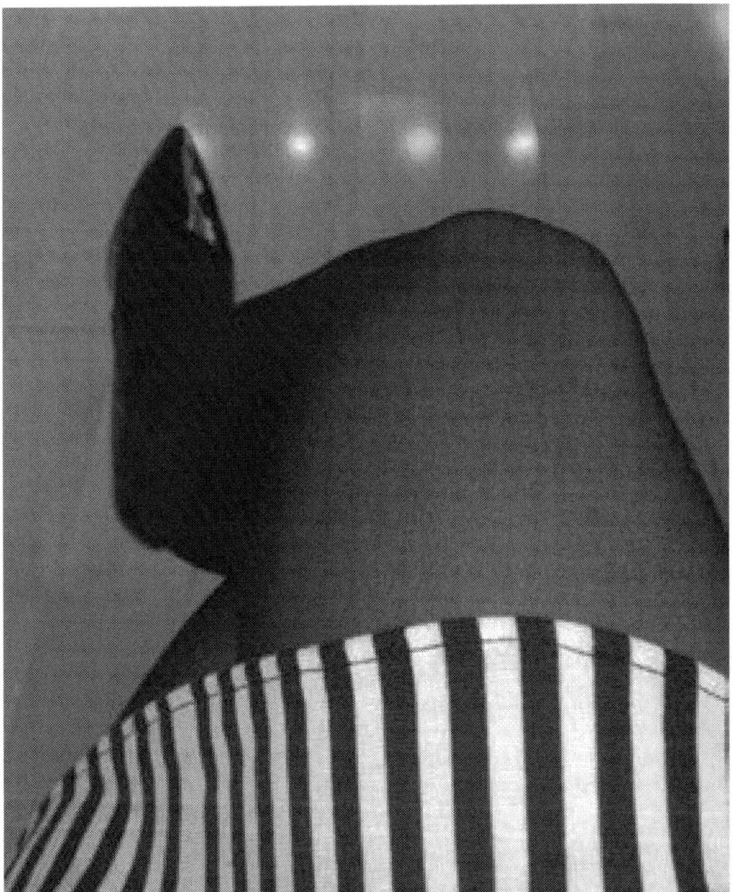

Rossana Campo was born in Genoa, Italy, in 1963 and divides her time between Rome and Paris. Her debut novel, *In principio erano le mutande*, published in 1992, later became a film by the same title directed by Anna Negri in 1999. Several novels followed, establishing her as one of the most interesting authors in contemporary Italian literature. Among them, *Il pieno di super* (Feltrinelli, 1993), *Mai sentita così bene* (Feltrinelli, 1995), *L'attore americano* (Feltrinelli, 1997), *Sono pazza di te* (Feltrinelli, 2001), *L'uomo che non ho sposato* (Feltrinelli, 2003), *Duro come l'amore* (Feltrinelli, 2005), *Più forte di me* (Feltrinelli, 2007), *Lezioni di arabo* (Feltrinelli, 2010), *Felice per quello che sei - Confessioni di una buddista emotiva* (Perrone, 2012), *Il posto delle donne* (Ponte alle Grazie, 2013), and *Fare l'amore* (Ponte alle Grazie, 2014). The *Rizzoli-Larousse Dictionary of World Literature* says: "In Rossana Campo's ironic and at times dramatic pages fragile misfits in search of stability sketch out a world of antiheroes, outcasts and oddballs, to whom the author's tender and disenchanted gaze imparts a vibrant humanity in a quotidian, incisive, colorful language." Campo's work has been translated into several languages, including French, Spanish, Dutch, German, Portuguese, Greek, and Romanian.

The following is an excerpt from *Mai sentita così bene*.

NEVER FELT SO GOOD

Rossana Campo

Should we break out the ice cream? Ale asks.

What kind did you get? Monica asks.

Häagen-Dazs, malaga and hazelnut.

Yuck, Nordic ice cream! Betty says, like some kind of know-it-all. How could you do such a thing? The best ice cream in the world is Italian!

Well excuse me, Nadia says, pissed, because she is precisely the kind of person who can't stand such observations.

Ladies! Monica goes, throwing her hands in the air. We're in Paris! All of us Italians hang out together, we always speak Italian, we eat Italian food . . . Give me a break!

But we hook up with foreigners, Nadia goes.

We've created a sort of Little Italy.

Yeah, well, I think the advantage of living abroad is that you can choose the Italians you want to hang with, but in Italy you have to deal with the whole bunch.

Plus Italian television! Nadia goes.

Shut up, you got cable just to watch the Italian evening news, Betty blurts out.

So? Nadia goes.

Ooh, bad sign, we're on the verge of the immigrant syndrome. We're willing to do anything to feel a little closer to the fatherland, even watch the TG1 news, Monica concludes, opening the ice cream.

Anyway, let's not get ourselves down thinking about depressing things, let's eat the ice cream and forget about it, I declare.

So, how do you do it? Nadia asks Monica, returning to the topic close to her heart.

Huh? Monica asks.

I mean, Nadia insists, do you really enjoy your extramar . . .

No, uh-uh, don't say that word because I hate it.

Extra what?

Shhhh, I go, when she gets pissed she's terrible.

No, seriously, how the hell do you do it?

Don't you ever fall in love?

Always, I always fall in love, every single time.

And you never think about leaving Paul?

If you ask me, you're a lot like Madame Bovary, Ale goes.

Madame Bovary c'est toi! Monica exclaims, irritated.

Well, I am faithful, Ale declares. I just can't cheat, I can't help it. I was raised that way, and there's not a damn thing I can do about it.

We were all raised that way, honey. But how about getting past that and taking a couple of baby steps on your own, know what I mean?

Know what I mean? Betty repeats.

You go to hell, Ale goes.

Why? Betty goes, turning beet red again.

No, no, I . . . I just can't do it. I mean, the minute I get the urge to cheat on someone it's a sign things aren't going so well anymore, it's a sign something has ended. Maybe I don't want to admit it to myself, but that's the way it is, Ale says.

Oh, it's always the same story, Monica goes.

But do you love your husband? Nadia asks.

Yes, I do, I'm fond of him, I think he's sweet. When he's in a good mood he's actually nice, and I like the way he fucks. Of course variation isn't his strong suit, but I like it. I fall for the guys I have affairs with too, but I definitely don't want to end my marriage or run off to Mexico with my lover like they do in the soaps, because I know that every lover who turns into a husband becomes a husband.

I'll have to write that down, Nadia goes.

Monica eats some more ice cream and continues: Plus, when you're alone it's such a pain, one way or the other you're always on the hunt for someone who wants to get serious, always afraid the guy just wants to have fun, it's eating you up inside, a thousand useless questions. My way, the domestic tranquility side is all taken care of, and the wild sex side too.

You kill me, Valeria goes. You're so cool, Monica!

Take it easy, otherwise it'll go to her head, I go.

In the beginning I tried, Monica continues, what do you think? I mean, to be a wife. Not the home-and-church type, no, but still going out, doing my own thing. Minus the affairs. Well, it didn't work, girls, I was bored, and he was getting bored being with a bored woman.

And then?

Then I said to myself, Moneek old girl, what's wrong with you? What is it about you that makes you different from other wives? Why are you bored and the others aren't?

And what did you tell yourself? Ale asks.

What did I tell myself? Girls, I looked around, I talked with other women, and it's not like the ever faithful were oozing joy and fulfillment from every pore. So I found an answer, at least an answer that works for me. I told myself, honey, nothing's wrong with you, it's the high fidelity marriage that doesn't work!

Great, Nadia goes.

Too easy, Ale goes.

You talk like a man, Betty goes.

Why should I talk like a woman?

Of course, men kept everything that doesn't involve paranoia for themselves and left us the worst, I go, sounding kind of like Betty Friedan in her early days.

You're all sitting there asking yourselves how a relationship should work, Monica continues, how you should act to make it work well, and you've never thought about acting in a way that makes your life work? Always thinking about relationships, what do I do to get him, what do I do to keep him, what do I do to make him dump the other woman. You never entertained the thought of asking yourselves, what can I do to make myself happy? To enjoy life to the max without sitting around beating myself up?

No, Betty says.

Hey, Moneek, chapeau, Nadia goes.

No, seriously, you kind of come across like a flake, but damn, you've really got your shit together, you sure do! I go.

Thanks a bunch, she goes.

Hey, Simone de Beauvoir's got nothing on you, Ale goes, attempting the irony card, but I'd say she lost the hand and she knows it.

I'm gonna say one more thing and then I'll drop it. I've learned that when I live my way, without following other people's rules, without trying to do what people generally think is right, or what everyone else does, things go really well, and I feel great!

Here, have some more wine, I say.

Let's toast! Valeria goes.

To not following the rules, Betty goes.

Oh Lord, Ale goes.

No, wait a minute, what about Paul? Don't you ever think about him? Whether he's feeling bad? Don't you give a damn about hurting him?

I told you, dumbass, Paul is a lot happier with me when I'm happy. And besides, I think fessing up is just a way to relieve your own guilty conscience.

And in a cruel way, to boot.

Out of sight, out of mind, Valeria pronounces.

That's so hypocritical, Nadia says.

Call it whatever the fuck you want, Monica goes, keep your cystitis and go on getting fleeced by your shrink.

What's cystitis got to do with it? Valeria goes.

No, I think it's something else, too, Ale goes. What I think is you don't work, you don't do a fucking thing all day, so you get bored and then you go around looking to get laid.

Better going around looking to get laid than working, I go.

She's right, Monica goes.

Thanks, I go.

No, really, I've never understood the bullshit people say about work. That women should find fulfillment in work, that if you work you have your own identity . . . Who's ever been fulfilled from work?

Eleonora Duse, Virginia Woolf.

By work I mean doing something you don't give a damn about.

Look, if you ask me it's not like that for men either.

They teach you that working makes you forget your paranoias, thanks a lot, you lose your mind, and you forget everything.

I don't work, Monica adds, but I walk in the parks, I go to the movies, the theater, I read, I bullshit with my girlfriends, I get laid . . . and frankly, I never felt so good!

Great, Ale goes.

No, wait, I get what she's saying.

Like, when I have sex with a guy it always feels like I have to choose between giving myself up or giving up a fuck. In the end I usually give myself up.

It must have something to do with that. Like, in my case I think, did I do the right thing, did I say the right thing? Am I the type of woman he'd like? And then little by little I end up trying to change myself accordingly.

The thing is, for me, I'm too hungry for love to let me be myself. That's why I have to choose between being myself or being loved.

Bullshit.

No, really, it's true.

Take you, Ale, Monica goes, since you started going with Gianni you've put on a ton of weight, you've started cooking and you're behind in your exams at the university.

The doorbell, Nadia goes.

Huh? Ale goes.

Someone's ringing the doorbell.

Ale gets up and says: Hey, what do you want to bet Lucia is here, go open the door, I have to pee, I can't hold it anymore.

Monica gets up and goes to the door. ■

Translated by Adria Frizzi and Traci Andrighetti

Mauro Casiraghi was born in Milan, Italy, in 1969. Mesmerized by the works of William Shakespeare, he decided he had to read the Bard in the original language. Thus he went to study English and Creative Writing at Concordia University, Montreal, where he wrote and published his first short stories in English. After receiving a degree that could hardly guarantee any job opportunity in his home country, he returned to Italy and settled down in Rome to become, against all odds, a successful scriptwriter for cinema and television. His first novel *La camera viola* (Fazi editore, 2007) won both the Premio Carver and the Premio Carlo Cassola. His latest publications include a book of short stories, *Cinque morti inutili*, a collection of interviews with Italian contemporary writers, *Interviste sull'arte di scrivere*, and the novel *Un chilo di cenere*. He is always happy to see his writing translated into English, the language that first sparked his love for literature.

The following short story is unpublished.

REQUIEM DELUXE

Mauro Casiraghi

We are traveling a hundred miles an hour. Look at that old man on the beat-up Fiat Panda, he cannot believe his eyes, he watches us speeding past him in the fast lane, he has never seen one of these go so fast. When his turn will come, perhaps one of my colleagues will give him a ride. A ride to the house of the dead, yes. Yet again, this is a luxury service, Mercedes E-Class, Sunrise Model, dark gray, five seater with automatic transmission and sequential Speedtronic, large side windows for a panoramic view of the coffin. Could be too expensive for the guy. Unless of course he is one of those who *pretend* to be poor, and then he keeps a thick roll of banknotes hidden in the coffee box, and when he dies he wants the funeral mass with the Bishop and the church bells tolling all over town, the slab of expensive Carrara marble with black and white grains, and the head of Christ in bronze on top, and his photograph where he is smiling with only half of his face because of that stroke he had six years ago, and at the bottom the writing in embossed letters *To Our Beloved Umberto in Perpetual Memory, His Wife and Children.* And many thanks for the inheritance.

Think about that. A lifetime of hard work, and then you leave all the money to others to enjoy. What a rip-off. If your relatives are good people and deserve it, okay, you may even accept it, but if they are a bunch of blood-sucking parasites you should come out of the grave and start slamming doors, lifting tables, whispering their names in the dark while they hide in terror under their beds until you give them a heart attack. What's the use? you may ask. Is it worth it? In the end you just lie there and don't care anymore, the seasons will pass over you one after the other, the earth spins around carrying you along like a dead weight, to be or not to be is no longer a problem. Or is it?

Ride to the house of the dead actually sounds good. It's got a ring to it. Next Saturday I'll suggest the guys in my band use it for a new song. Who knows, maybe we'll get something out of it. In the past six months I've been singing the same shit, I'm sick and tired of it. Actually I'm sick and tired of everything. Sometimes it feels like I'm living through the dead days of a dead season in a dead country that nobody really cares to bring back to life. The only thing I still like is to drive fast early in the morning through the mist rising up from the ditches. The primordial dawn had to be more or less like this. A flat blanket of fog over the plain, no mountains or hills, just a clean slate. This is the foundation, where it all started. And that's where I'm coming from, darting like a bullet over the Padana Plain to make up for the time I lost. Yes, because no one ever stops to lend a hand if you get a flat tire with one of these. Drivers just look and pass by, clutching their balls to keep the bad luck away.

It's six forty-five now, and the funeral is at ten, which means that I still have three hours and fifteen minutes. To get to Florence will take nearly three hours, so I can't slow down even a second, even if I have to piss I have to hold it because being on time is the first thing and this is a first-class service, yes, Madam, a real luxury service. Do not worry, Madam, you go back to Florence to make the funeral arrangements, we're going to take care of transportation, by the way this young man here is the driver in charge of translating the body. My pleasure. My pleasure, Madam, condolences, my sympathy and my pleasure, it's really a pleasure to make your acquaintance. Oh yes, it was really a great pleasure to meet her. You lucky bastard, where did you find a woman like that? Come on, don't be offended, I mean it as a compliment. If you were still with us I would never dare to say it, but in the intimacy of our trip I feel I should be completely honest with you. I confess that I really like your widow, she must be at least ten years older than me but she's still beautiful, and yes, if I had the chance and the opportunity I would not hesitate to take your place. After all, it's quite common when you lose someone that you develop a great need for comforting and understanding. Don't get me wrong, I don't usually do this kind of thing, taking advantage of the emotional state of a widow after a loss is against my principles, I'm a professional, and I have the utmost respect for those in mourning. But the thing is that she is just the kind of woman that makes me lose my head, I have the feeling that with a woman like that I could actually do something good with my life, so I guess I'm saying that it would not be a fleeting thing, if there were the premises and the opportunities and an actual development, and if she too wanted it very strongly, well, I won't deny that I'd give her all my comforting and all my understanding and I would do my best to make her forget you as soon as possible.

You'll agree with me that the idea that we should remember the dead forever and ever is the perversion of a much more natural feeling: respect for the past. One thing is to be faithful to your personal history, remembering where you came from and who was on your side as a traveling companion; another thing is to live bound to everlasting love and devotion to someone who no longer exists and whom we do not allow ourselves to ever forget. Take my grandmother for example. We don't have time now, otherwise I would take the Casalpusterlengo exit, and I'd show you this small village on the north bank of the Po River that I'm sure you never heard of. My grandma was born there and spent a hellish childhood with a horrible stepmother who, whenever she wet the bed at night, made her run around the streets with the dirty sheets on her head for everyone to see. She grew up cherishing the memory of her real mother who was a very beautiful woman (grandma used to show me the old black-and-white photograph where her mother posed with a long white dress and the placid look of someone who has already figured out most things since she knows she doesn't have much time left), until the day she met my grandfather who sang arias from operettas, and when he was a child he used to be in the chorus of Toscanini, and he'd walk home all the way from La Scala barefoot with his Sunday shoes in hand to save the soles. My grandmother was not even fifteen when she let him take her away from the village, she ran away from the horrible stepmother and was happy with her husband for seven years, they had two daughters and built a house and had a future together, until the day my grandfather stopped singing arias because of throat cancer, and he was not even thirty when he got his marble slab to Eternal Memory and his photograph closed in a locket on my grandmother's chest, that chest that no other man was ever to caress and kiss again. After her daughters and grandchildren grew up, there was nothing left for her to do, except to dedicate herself to the eternal memory of her husband. She never failed to visit his grave every Sunday, and we all thought she was living in peace, with her mother's look in the eyes, the look of someone who has understood most things and has accepted them all as one accepts the rising sun and the falling rain, and then finally one day her day came too, she was lying in the hospital bed clutching the locket with his photograph, and we all thought, well, in a little while the two of them will be together again, feeling a little less sad about her imminent departure, when all of a sudden my grandmother sits up from the bed and tries to rip the locket from her neck shouting in rage and regret, *Damn you! Curse you! All those years I wasted! Curse you that have left me so soon! Donkey head you are!* That's what she said cursing him in dialect, *Quand te se mort ti son mort anca mi, I died on the day you died, you asshole!* We were all pretty shocked. After her death nobody dared to talk about it, but I'm sure that every time someone from my family goes to the cemetery where my grandparents were buried side by side they cannot help thinking what kind of life they had and how short-lived was their happiness, at least that's what I think when I'm there at the tomb after I dust the marble and clean the gravel and put fresh flowers for them. It's all a huge rip off, that's what I think. Don't you agree?

After Bologna the traffic is increasing a bit, but today there won't be many people around, it's too cold to go to the beach, and the snow has not yet arrived in the mountains, maybe I can make it on time. Now the Padana Plain is finished, and we're riding on top of the hills, this sweet up and down is like a bass rhythm, *stump, stump, stump, take a ride, take a ride, from the cradle to the bed,* it could actually turn out to be a cool song, I must remember to jot down the words otherwise tomorrow I'll forget everything. Moments of true inspiration are very rare, and if you don't act upon them and let too much time go by, after a while they seem ridiculous, there's that particular moment when you have some important things to say and would do anything to be able to say them, but two hours later you start to wonder if they are really so important and if anyone would ever give a shit, the magic moment is gone and it is as if it never came, the idea that carried such deep and urgent meaning is now like an empty shell, and from there I usually go down in free fall towards that feeling of nothingness that leaves scars on me like after an accident or a bad disease, scars that no one can see and no one knows about because I never tell anyone anything. Anyone except you, of course, and the others like you when I drive them to your final destination. At this point I could say that after all you are better off than me, you won't have to face such crisis ever again, like when suddenly the blood pumps stronger and stronger in the neck veins, the back of my head gets cold and tight, I put my hands on my knees and say slowly, okay, now stop running and face one by one all the dilemmas that sooner or later you have to face, starting with the simple ones like, *What am I doing here why don't I do myself in right now?* up to the mind-boggling questions that relate to time and space and the Creator of the Universe, who on the last day will come down and destroy the earth in fire and judge the living and the dead. I'm talking about all those moments of lonely terror that fill me with desire to hang myself from a beam or hide under the covers and go to sleep and never wake up again. But I won't. I won't say that you're better off than me. Maybe your soul flew up to heaven in the midst of saints and is now singing with the choir of angels who never get a wrong note, while I keep rehearsing the same shitty songs with my group of nerds stuck in a basement with no one listening to us, but the fact remains that you're lying back there in a coffin, and this trip to the cemetery is the last thing that will happen to you, while I can still shoot at a hundred miles an hour out of the primordial dawn, I can still get to Florence in time for your funeral even if I got a flat tire at the start, I can still give my condolences to your widow, hold her hand, smell her perfume, dream to kiss her and touch her thighs under her black dress, I can make up a song and sing it with my friends or alone in the car like an idiot, *Take a ride, take a ride, from the cradle to the bed, take a ride to the house of the dead,* and that's how it is, and that's how it will be until the end of time, so relax, my friend, enjoy the journey, and rest in peace, amen. ■

Translated by the author

Ernesto Livorni is professor of Italian language and literature, and affiliate of comparative literature, at the University of Wisconsin–Madison. His scholarly publications include *Avanguardia e tradizione: Ezra Pound e Giuseppe Ungaretti* (Le Lettere, 1998) and *T. S. Eliot, Montale e la modernità dantesca* (forthcoming). He also translated into Italian and edited Ted Hughes, *Cave-Birds: Un dramma alchemico della caverna* (2001). He has published articles in Italian and in English on medieval, modern, and contemporary Italian literature, English and American literature, Italian-American literature, and comparative literature. Livorni is the founding editor of *L'Anello che non tiene: Journal of Modern Italian Literature*. Livorni has also published three collections of poems: *Prospettiche illusioni* (1977-1983) (Tracce, 1987), *Nel libro che ti diedi. Sonetti* (1985-1986) (Campanotto,1998), and *L'America dei Padri* (Manni, 2005). The collection *Onora il Padre e la Madre*, which gathers previously published and new poems, is forthcoming.

The following "Coded Message" appeared in *Steve. Rivista di poesia*, 37, Autunno 2009. "The Widow's Dream" appeared in *Frontiera*, n.4, settembre 1996. "Playing Dead" is unpublished.

CODED MESSAGE

Ernesto Livorni

Opening up the bag, a book
in code and in the book
a message of yours: "You will miss us!"
How much vanity in one's heart,
how much verity in the letter,
which begins your name and ends
my self-importance.

Translated by Jacob Blakesley

THE WIDOW'S DREAM

Ernesto Livorni

The jacket hangs from the branch, shorn
of your figure, black in the shade
of the bare tree; the dark tanned leather
of your briefcase: seeing you
among the relics of the journey, no
consolation remains on our path.
I hear you moaning on the branch, taut
under the weight of your clothes; no wind
creaks in the hollow trunk of hours,
no termite, mole, or mouse gnaws on
your essence; you wail inside the atrium
of my heart, that vain, dissonant harp
which mixes in my stomach the breath
of decay with your wine-filled blood.
I hear you wailing, and you no longer wander
as a trembling shadow in the plow-traced
furrow, plowshare and lump of earth.

And yet you appear to me; truly alive, you
appear to me, smiling: were you waiting for me? I
certainly was, ever since you departed at that hour
without a jacket or bag; do you see them there
on the branch and at the bottom of the deep-rooted stump?
In the ecstasy of that time still remaining
among dear things I regard them
and among the worn-out badges I pray
for your peace, peace for the frayed
fabric, peace for the veined leather.
But you do not speak, you come near:
where do you come from? Does your breath
which greets us repose in the hollow tree?
Do you sink your steps into the roots,
mingle clots of dirt and lymph?

You are silent. I call to you, but you do not respond to me;
instead you come towards the bag
full of documents, newspapers, records
of a forgotten time, confused
with the other fragments of that day of yours:
the bottle of wine, the bread-basket.
Bent over the soil, digging in the bulge
of that bag, I hear your wail:
you raise your forehead with a proud gaze,
and you lift up loose sheets, green ink,
throbbing with tears. Speak, tell me:
are they letters, leisurely composed,
buried then at the end of the journey?
Poems? You look at me with your smile
quivering with emotion: poems,
and may they be the eternal legacy of the emotion
that the heart grants to the living.
Your hand is warm, as in the final
instant: I hear you wailing, you are silent,
last verse of the pulse's rhythm.

Translated by Jacob Blakesley

PLAYING DEAD

Ernesto Livorni

The dead body floats, his eyes
dazzled in the sun, the waves
dampen the tuft of hair inside his ear.
This is the art of open
arms, ready for the empty
embrace, the constant risk
of the other. Liquid motion
impassively entrusted to the waves.

Between what is said
and what is done,
there is an ocean;
between being and acting,
life gives its all,
revealing itself
in a body's contours.
Conclusive experience
unexperienced (death, birth)
amid, yes, life.

Children are stamping in the surf:
playing dead is an art
too lively to drown.

Translated by Jacob Blakesley

MOON THROUGH CYPRESS OAKS

Rudi Dundas

Gabriele Pedullà (Rome, 1972) teaches Italian Literature at the University of Rome 3. His first collection of short stories, *Lo spagnolo senza sforzo* (Einaudi, 2009) won the "Premio Mondello Opera Prima," the "Premio Verga," the "Premio Frontino," and the "Premio Grisi." In 2010 he was selected by *Il Sole 24 Ore* literary supplement as one of the ten best Italian fiction writers under 40. His nonfiction work *In Broad Daylight: Movies and Spectators after the Cinema* is available in English (Verso, 2012). His first novel, *Lame*, will be published by Einaudi in early 2016.

The short story presented here appears in *Lo spagnolo senza sforzo*.

MIRANDA

Gabriele Pedullà

Rays of light are to the eyes as canes are to the hands,
and the eye may be likened to an organ with an infinite
number of hands holding onto an infinite number of canes.
ÉTIENNE BONNOT DE CONDILLAC, *Treatise on the Sensations*

The first time Miranda suggests they go shopping together they're sitting down to the umpteenth cappuccino that morning at the university cafe, and Stefi obviously replies with a quick yes, even though she notices a hint of embarrassment in her tone that irks her, embarrassment, although why should there be, there's nothing about a question like that that should embarrass her, but even at the not-so-tender age of twenty-two everything new still scares her, which must be why her father still calls her my little girl, even in public and even at the not-so-tender age of twenty-two, to anyone else Stefi's still his little girl (that's just how dad is, everybody knows).

Shopping with Miranda—Stefi's never thought about it, but it's normal that two friends, so totally normal, like talking about clothes or boys or new movies (although movies are out of the question, at least with Miranda), yet Stefi's anxious just the same, and now kind of upset that Miranda will have noticed her untimely hesitation, because she has real feelers when it comes to certain things, and always picks up on everything (even if you'd never think so). She doesn't know how she does it, she senses them, she simply senses them, and Stefi's certain that in this case Miranda will have measured the three seconds of silence between her question and the answer with that natural metronome hidden in her ear, which doesn't skip a beat, by now she knows her pretty well, so basically her affirmative answer, a yes, but somehow anxious and uncertain, also in light of the fact that Stefi's never been any good at lying to her friends. Come on, it'll be fun, Miranda quickly adds, as if to encourage her, giving her a little extra shot of trust, although Stefi's already rebounded, and replies in turn with a yes of course, of course, which already sounds more persuasive, especially because of her tone of voice. Of course Miranda, fantastic, really, I can't wait.

That's not actually how it is, but at this point she might as well fake it, a skill Stefania has never really mastered since all it takes is a little white lie for her mouth to start smiling on its own, like some unruly little schoolgirl trying in vain to cover up the evidence. It's too bad though, because Stefi guesses, no, actually, she's sure that Miranda has detected her embarrassment and she's saddened by it, no matter how much she keeps telling herself that it's no different, she's well aware that that isn't the case, and it pains her, always. She always wishes things were different between them, basically she wishes there were no difference at all (at least between the two of them), and yet all it takes is the slightest distraction and once again the worst prejudices gain the upper hand, even now, even with her, because it's unbelievable but in the end Stefi reacted exactly like anyone else would have, and now she's ashamed. What a wuss. So typical.

The fact is, Miranda's blind, or, as one should say in such cases, to be more PC (and, indeed, as Stefi always says, because she's so careful about such things), visually impaired. How many times has she had to tell her parents and sister not to use that word? But now it seems they, too, have finally learned, and they, too, say the visually impaired friend of our dear Stefi, it's longer but decidedly more appropriate, decidedly nicer. Of course Stefania would be no less interested in Miranda if Miranda were to have 20/20 vision. Not even Giorgio would make such a mean accusation, and sometimes he can be a real jerk (you'd think he does it on purpose just to annoy her) but it's also true that Stefi has gained a reputation as a relentless do-gooder. Everyone says so, she's so involved in the sentimental preoccupations of her friends, ever ready to lend a hand, just say the word and she's on it, because, between global warming and Mrs. Pellegrini's newborn kittens who need to be put up for adoption, there's a whole world out there in need of saving, it's right there just waiting for her. Animals, human beings, plants . . . what difference does it make? Just don't get in her way, don't trip up her obsessive need to right all the wrongs and iron out all injustice! In such cases, trying to make her reason becomes a pipe dream. Just ask Giorgio. It's a fixation, a real fixation (and he laughs, with that laugh of his that's a bit feminine, which Stefi doesn't find so pleasant). Maybe it really is because Stefi's always had it so easy (the right family, the right schools, the right boyfriend), pretty much everything comes to her all too easily, but those are just Giorgio's classic jokes, comments that always annoy her so much. Softy, softy, hey Florence Nightingale, who'd you save today? Thank God for Stefi! Yup, Giorgio sure can be odious when he puts his mind to it.

Before meeting Miranda in one of their grad-level journalism classes, Stefania already knew who she was because they'd often crossed paths on campus, and also because of the many rumors she'd heard, the countless unpleasant anecdotes she couldn't help but overhear. It's unbelievable how little her classmates like her, Stefi thinks—the blind chick did this, the blind chick did that—so many implausible stories of her rudeness and arrogant ripostes in which everybody refers to her as the blind chick, so straightforwardly, almost as if Miranda didn't have a first and last name like everyone else. The blind chick, the blind chick, the blind chick: unbearable. When she's around no one dares display such disrespect, go figure, but their classmates do all they can to steer clear of her, you can see that right away, maybe because she's better than most of them (and doesn't hide the fact that she knows it), even though she can't see. Or maybe because of her reputation for being an acerbic and surly young woman (a detail that, at least according to Stefi, isn't far off the mark).

Anyone who knows Stefi knows that even less than that would've sufficed to pique her curiosity and trigger her predictable and self-gratifying impulse toward solidarity, her eternal battle to defend the less fortunate, the marginalized, one of Stefi's hallmarks from high school onward, even though the demands of earning her master's degree forced her to give up volunteering, and even though her various classes and her Russian homework leave her almost no free time, not even for seeing friends. For a few months she'd spotted her in one classroom or another, and at the department cafe, as Miranda sipped her orange juice, earbuds invariably glued to her head as if to shut out the outside world, I can't see you and I don't even want to hear you, leave me alone, the message in such cases was utterly apparent. In other words, she was pretty much always by herself. After all, even without all those rumors, you couldn't help but notice someone like Miranda around LUISS's well-manicured campus. Not so much because of the dark glasses she wears, even at night and when it's raining, even during class, or because of her guide dog, a pitch-black lab so big that some people are afraid of him despite his large, friendly, trusty-dog eyes, but more because of her overall effect. The way she dresses would be enough on its own, for example, her flawless, maniacal, perennial attention to detail, because Miranda certainly stands out from the rest of the students simply by what she wears, decidedly too fancy compared to their peers' standards, in skirts, complete with jewelry, for example, or her makeup, sometimes quite elaborate (jewelry and makeup, mini- and maxi-skirts), with an attention to detail quite rare even for LUISS, such a far cry from the flophouse of La Sapienza, where the students wear the craziest things, and, as Stefi's father likes to say, life is just one big year-round carnival. But Stefi doesn't count, she's also called out for caring too much about her looks, an old-fashioned girl is the way her more generous peers put it, but it's only because she likes to feel at ease with her body, wearing the right clothes for the right occasion, just a simple string of pearls when necessary, or a trip to the hairdresser and a massage at that place just around the corner from Piazza Euclide, without splurging like Carlotta and Lavinia have, who've become obsessed with massages over the past few months. Feeling at ease with one's own body, that's all.

Whereas Stefi has a large scarf collection, adores her big brother's sweaters, and doesn't wear high heels, Miranda, who's banished suits from her wardrobe once and for all in favor of form-fitting pants and short skirts, goes for a slightly showier, more provocative look. It's not just the five-year age difference between them, but no one would ever describe Miranda as an old-fashioned girl, and it's not just because of the super-tall boots that make her look even slimmer and more feminine as she strolls around campus with that sensual, slightly swaying strut of hers that you can't help but notice (the snide remarks Stefania has heard about it take a rather different tone). Maybe she's a bit of an exhibitionist? Before getting to know her Stefi thought so—especially because of those mini-skirts, so short, so impractical for class—but without any resentment or sense of aversion.

They didn't become friends right away and even now you could say they're just at the beginning. Stefi only points that out because she knows from experience how rare and precious friendship is, how delicate, how real feelings take time, and with Miranda it was all so quick and unexpected, so unforeseen and therefore all the more welcome. For now, after four months, Stefi just likes to think they're on the right path: they'll become friends, she's sure. Now, for example, it sounds unbelievable, but if it weren't for that sociology exam they might never have spoken to one another. Partially it's because Stefi is generally shy, everyone knows, even if, when push comes to shove, she does know how to bare her teeth—as Giorgio always says, watch out for the quiet ones, the quiet ones are the most dangerous—but what really counted was Miranda's bad rep for being nasty, snooty, and thinking back on it now it's obvious, the fact that Miranda can't see has nothing to do with her peers' revulsion, it's actually that superior, vaguely disdainful air of hers, her slightly arrogant behavior that's alienated everyone. Or at least that's how Stefi seems to have understood it.

And so, up until they actually spoke, even Stefania was under the impression that Miranda was dismissive of her, but even that piqued her curiosity a bit, you can't deny that such a dogged animosity toward the whole universe exuded a certain allure for someone like Stefi, a master of Freudianisms who's invariably intrigued by the labyrinths of the psyche and the kind of negation that suddenly and magically morphs into the most brilliant kind of consent. As if she didn't know that sometimes compassion is worse than outright offense! Actually, in terms of Miranda's bearing, which never aims to inspire sympathy nor expects any special treatment, Stefi doesn't find anything particularly unusual, nothing she hadn't already come across repeatedly as a volunteer when she was in high school, beginning with that clear refusal to butter you up, that almost programmatic toughness, even when it meant coming across as unpleasant and stand-offish to anyone lacking the patience to look just a bit beyond the surface.

But it's also true that sometimes she goes overboard. Stefi's pained by all the malicious talk surrounding Miranda because Miranda's her friend, or she's becoming her friend, but despite that she can't exactly say their peers are wrong, and once she even suggested, albeit very carefully (because you never know how Miranda will read into your words, so it's always best to tread lightly), you should be a bit kinder with them, she told her, you're too defensive, it's not like they're all out to get you. Wasted breath. Too defensive? Miranda unleashed her usual sarcasm. Don't fall for it, they're only nice to me because I'm blind so they think I'll be an easy lay, tits and ass up for grabs, sweetie, that's it, that's all I am to those guys, was Miranda's irritated answer, complete with her usual sexual explicitness, which always made Stefi a bit uncomfortable, because unlike Miranda she was brought up rather rigidly in that regard, an upbringing that caused problems every now and then with Giorgio (but everyone knows how guys are and anyway, there are certain things she just won't do).

Sometimes Miranda's downright impossible, thinks Stefi, in these cases with a hint of reproach, but she must've suffered so much, who knows what she's been through to speak this way, because otherwise she'd never talk like that, tits and ass up for grabs, an expression that gives her goosebumps. And so, when she sees someone step aside in the hallway to let her pass more easily and without impediment, Stefi can't help but think that, in reality, they are avoiding her, it isn't kindness or consideration, it's fear. From what's become of the few people, mostly males, who've tried to break through the invisible barrier that

Miranda's built around herself, Stefi doesn't really feel she can blame them all that much. Tits and ass up for grabs, geez. With crude replies like that, sometimes Miranda manages to scare even her.

It sort of bothers her to know she's so alone. Not that she seems it at first, because at a glance you're drawn in, even in her state Miranda could get any guy, absolutely any guy she wanted, Stefania has no doubt, because you can see how they all watch her, even out on the street and not just because of Argo or the dark glasses she wears even at night, and yet on campus she doesn't connect with anyone, she just charges ahead, straight as an arrow, which is also undeniably the most striking aspect of Miranda's temperament—her forceful character, strong enough to plough through any and every obstacle without worrying even slightly about the consequences. Now that they're becoming friends, though, Stefi's beginning to see Miranda a bit differently. Indeed, after overcoming her initial surprise, Stefania really likes the idea of going shopping together, friendships need a degree of normality and little things like this, shopping or massages or going swimming together, just like with all her other friends. What's more, Miranda's eye for fashion has always intrigued her, it's both smart and elegant yet at the same time trendy, aside from a clear preference for black, enlivened by a touch of color, of course, because all it takes is a splash, a scarf, or a pair of shoes, or maybe a little jewelry to break up the monotony of dark monochromes, a sensitivity even Miranda seems to have learned to perfection.

A visually impaired girl who's invariably dressed to the nines isn't the first thing you'd expect, and indeed, in the beginning Stefi thought a pair of doting parents or a devoted boyfriend were there for her (most likely a boyfriend, a boyfriend would've explained a lot), so ever since she learned that Miranda's family lives in Macerata and that she's all on her own in Rome, without anyone to look after her, Stefi is even more struck by her taste in fashion. Her color pairings, for example: those color pairings remain the main mystery. If she were more easygoing she'd probably already have asked: your outfits, how do you choose them? Stefi never sheds her fear of hurting people with an out-of-place remark, though, especially with people in Miranda's condition you have to be extra careful, and because she doesn't know how Miranda will take such a question she's always avoided broaching the topic.

Miranda, on the other hand, doesn't seem to worry so much. Stefi vividly recalls the very first time they spoke, between their sociology and international relations classes there's always an hour break and Stefi was going over her lecture notes when she heard someone blurt out, Are you Stefania? Just like that, no intro or anything, because

Miranda had been absent from the last lecture and their professor had suggested she be in touch with the tall blonde girl who sits in the front row (presuming such words would make sense to Miranda), yes, exactly, the one who had asked about Veblen shortly before, the tall blonde girl in the front row who recorded every class and so maybe she could help out. Miranda didn't waste any time: would you be so kind as to help me out? The professor told me you record every lecture—I'd need last Thursday's. That was it. It was not so much a question as an order, at least judging from the bossy, slightly authoritarian tone with which she said it, leaving no chance to answer, in keeping with the countless rumors about her. But requests for help, brusque or otherwise, are never an issue for Stefi, quite the contrary. And so they arranged and carried out the exchange without much formality, a week later Miranda had given the recording back to Stefi and it ended there, with a simple thanks in a plain yet not impolite tone, thanks, I really appreciate it, and that was it, not a word more nor less. But from then on Miranda had always said hi, sometimes rather warmly, and Stefi then realized for the first time that Miranda had her own unique way of detecting who entered or exited a room, a talent for tapping into sounds or magnetic fields that never fails to amaze her, especially since even now Stefi doesn't get how she always seems to know where she's sitting and walk right up to her, even if she hasn't so much as opened her mouth.

Becoming friends took a bit longer, it was Miranda who suggested they work on their sociology papers together, but Stefi didn't hesitate, despite what Giorgio says her vocation as a modern-day Florence Nightingale played no role in this case, because Miranda is one of the best in the class, hands-down the best (quite likely), even though she has to do all the work with audiobooks and transcriptions that are sometimes delivered late or incomplete, so that of course, all told, it's not the same thing. Sure, the computer is a huge help, with programs that immediately translate standard texts into braille and vice versa, allowing her to write her papers just like everyone else. According to what Stefi's said, it's real sci-fi stuff. Up until a few weeks ago she had no idea how much technology had improved the lives of the visually impaired, for example that cellphone setting that automatically transforms text messages into voicemail, or GPS that lets you navigate even the most labyrinthine city without the help of a white cane or a guide dog. Sure, those must be a major help. Yet all that wouldn't mean a thing without real willpower, Stefi keeps repeating that she's never met anyone so determined, so tenacious, someone with Miranda's character is bound to get what she wants in life. Now that she's decided to become a radio journalist Stefi has no doubt she'll manage it (for sure), because if there's anyone who deserves to hit the bull's-eye it's definitely Miranda.

Miranda and Stefania as a classic case of opposites attract? They seem to fit the bill, as Giorgio quips: you're blonde and she's brunette, you're shy and she's arrogant, you can see and she's blind. Stefi doesn't laugh along with him and strains to keep her mouth shut, it's better to ignore him when he says stuff like that, all the more so since, despite Giorgio and his idiotic comments, their decision to write their sociology paper together turned out to be a major success, and going shopping together will be a good way to celebrate their A+ grades from the toughest professor in the whole department. Stefi's parents, on the other hand, took an immediate liking to Miranda, and to Argo, too, because once you meet him you can't possibly be afraid of him, he's so sweet, so tame, and even though Stefi's mother usually doesn't let pets into the house it's clear she doesn't mind making an exception for Argo and Miranda. That evening Giorgio can't hide his amusement. Now it's shopping with Batgirl, what'll it be next? He says solely to tick Stefi off. Just like two girly girls, he jeers, remember that afterward we're having dinner at Duke's with Ludovico and Arianna, so please don't be late again this time, okay? Then he adds: if this Miranda of yours is as cute as you say she is, we should introduce her to Marco, don't you think? Only a true Batgirl could go for a dog like him. And he laughs harder, with that sour, slightly girly laugh of his that Stefi finds increasingly difficult to take. Giorgio calls her Batgirl thinking it's cute. How's Batgirl? he asks, and you'd think even Stefi would find it funny, even though she's told him a million times that she can't stand that joke, making fun of others' misfortunes is low, something only mean kids would do, but he keeps at it, no bad blood intended, it's just for the sake of breaking the rules a bit and putting her on edge. She totally regrets that time she rebuked him, saying it's not nice to call her blind, Stefi recalls, because blind is a rude term, and ever since then Giorgio does nothing but repeat the same mocking remark, if she isn't blind then she must be Batgirl, it seems obvious to him, and calling her visually impaired solely to please Stefi is totally out of the question. Look it up, Stefi tells him, irritated and with an edge of meanness this time, a tone she rarely takes with Giorgio, and anyway you should know that bats aren't completely blind, everybody knows that.

Luckily the week flies by and soon it's Friday. Stefania shows up punctually at Piazza Colonna, she'd never make her wait, but Miranda's already there, without Argo. Stefi takes it as yet more proof that she still can't know exactly what to expect. Will she come with Argo or without him? Which stores should they go to? How much should she plan to walk? It's questions like these that have stressed her out all morning, although upon seeing Miranda she feels a bit calmer, almost serene. And what a sunny day. Rome is particularly bright today, and in the thrill of this first little taste of spring the comment slips out of Stefania's mouth without much thought, and then she immediately worries whether what she's said is okay or whether she's tripped up again, whether talking about brightness with Miranda might be another major faux pas, just the latest in a long line of gaffes. Way to go, Stefi, we're off to a great start, and already she begins to regret her words. She'll be more careful, by now it's pretty clear: with Miranda you really have to stay on your toes.

Yet the day really does have a surprising brightness to it, just yesterday it was winter, drab, and today, all of a sudden the sun shines on everyone's starved skin for the first time, you can feel it, it's pretty much the perfect day for a pair of friends to go shopping, already looking ahead to bikinis and the beach, a seasonal passion for heading out to the islands that Stefi always talks about in way too much detail, if it weren't for Miranda piping up that no, she prefers the mountains, and she hasn't gone to the beach since she was fifteen. Of course it's just a matter of personal preference, and the episode doesn't detract in the least from the euphoria they feel thanks to the light and unexpectedly early warmth in the air, they're still in the thrall of that contagious excitement that comes with the first day of spring. Now their next step will be to leave behind the chaos on Via del Corso to explore the little side streets, all the best boutiques are there, and since they're already in the area they might as well stop in at Sant'Eustachio, but just for an espresso, Stefi says, since summer's coming and she's already vowed that she'd give up sweets for a month, including the amazing espresso granita topped with whipped cream, their specialty. Shall we? Miranda takes her arm and need not even say a word, they stroll along, arm-in-arm yet at a swift clip, as Stefi grows increasingly intrepid, gaining an almost immediate and natural steadiness in step with Miranda's particular stride—her rather singular way of slinking down the street as if she's almost dancing, which never ceases to amaze Stefi.

Not that Stefi's all that calm, actually. For now they're headed toward the Pantheon but she still doesn't really get exactly what it means to go shopping with Miranda, it certainly won't be anything like shopping with Lavinia or Carlotta, it can't be the same as with her other friends, because with them she always just wanders around with no set destination, browsing the window displays and stopping at whim, they rarely go in and it's even rarer that they try something on, it's all so casual and so free, no plans, just following impulse, which is after all what's so nice about shopping, that infinite freedom to let yourself go amid a million different possibilities before stumbling across the one belt that perfectly matches that short mid-season coat Giorgio gave her for her birthday. But with Miranda? Stefi doesn't even know if she has anything precise in mind, or whether she just wants to have a look around (yet another unfortunate phrase, one to banish from her vocabulary, because language sure doesn't help in the battle she's waging to adapt her words to fit Miranda's world), but at least she can use this little break to carefully suss out what it is Miranda's thinking. And so she asks her, stealthily licking the last traces of whipped cream and granita from her upper lip (and anyway, Miranda can't see her): Is there a particular kind of store you'd like to check out?

As soon as Miranda utters the word shoes Stefi proposes four or five different places, all nearby and all apparently very special, super trendy, hot spots, as Stefi likes to say, using the English terms, expressing herself with the young-sounding, hip, Americanized lingo she couldn't do without when talking about make-up and clothes, especially when she's with her friends, since as soon as she's with her mom the adjectives she uses are much more traditional. Luckily Miranda, too, hates those super-pointy styles that were in fashion a couple years back, the ones Stefi couldn't stand either. So when Miranda asks her if it happens to be one of those kinds of shops, Stefi's happy to reassure her it isn't, no way, I'd never take you to one of those places, and an instant later she's even happier to have a laugh at her joke about the irrefutable relationship between those oversized pointy toes and Freud's undisputed theories about phallic symbols and penis envy. She does adore high heels, Miranda is quick to specify, she's loved them ever since she was a teenager, even if, for someone like her, flats would be better, little or no heel, more suitable and safer, too, above all since in her case heels could potentially cause real balance issues. Stefi nods. Still, Miranda continues, that doesn't have to be the case, you know, and all it takes is a little practice, where there's a will there's a way, even if Rome's cobblestones sure don't make it the easiest place to face such challenges. You're telling me, says Stefi, echoing the sentiment, although her timing's a little off. Yeah, on cobblestones heels drive me totally nuts.

Glancing around Stefi immediately sees that the palette this spring will be cream and orange, it's clear from the first few window displays, but she's sorry she can't share this discovery with Miranda. With her arm hooked around Stefi's, Miranda stands out less than she does with Argo, but it's still pretty obvious, with the exception of one rude kid who's sprinting by and almost knocks her to the ground, virtually everyone notices right away that Miranda can't see, so they're more careful. If anything Stefi's actually annoyed by all the attention, since she isn't used to having so many eyes aimed in her direction and she had no idea (but who knows if you can really get used to something like that), the way they look at her, and the whispered comments, as if encountering a visually impaired girl was something so out of the ordinary. What're you lookin' at? Stefi keeps thinking, irritated by the umpteenth indiscreet glance, because especially now that they've paused in front of the windows of the second shop and Miranda's asked her to describe the shoes, everybody's staring at them. In this case it's her immobility that gives it away, or, more precisely, the contrast between Stefi's movement and Miranda's stone-cold stillness, her head facing out far above, like someone whose eyes aren't really taking in the people and things around them. She seems unnatural, distant, and come to think of it now, Stefi realizes that this posture of hers is another thing that makes Miranda seem so aloof and haughty to anyone who doesn't really know her, suddenly Stefi's certain that the hatred Miranda inspires in their classmates comes from exactly that, aside from her brusqueness, the coldness of their peers must come from their misinterpreting her physical way of being in space: basically, yet another misunderstanding.

That must be it. On the other hand, though, it's also true that with Miranda the salespeople are even kinder. Stefi is no stranger, she's a good, no, a great regular, she and her sister, no joke, over the past few years they've spent a small fortune here, not to mention her mother and her aunt from Trent, who makes a point of stopping in every time she comes down to Rome. Ah, what a lady, of course, how could they ever forget such a distinguished woman? Please, next time you speak to her, send her my regards, okay? As soon as they notice Miranda can't see, which is pretty much the instant Stefi walks through the door, the salesgirls heap on extra attention, and a minute later even the shop owner pops up, insisting she herself would like to look after them. Have they got their eye on anything in particular? Some new boots have just come in from Turin, if they'll be so kind as to wait just a moment Fabiola will go fetch them from storage, it won't take but a moment. They're as light and delicate as a glove, perfect for when it gets a bit warmer. How does she know? Well, it's obvious, it's so clear that Miranda's a boot-wearing kind of woman, you don't have to know her to figure that out, since it's all a matter of body type, with legs like that you pretty much have to wear short skirts and boots, take it from me, I've been doing this for thirty years, and trust me, in your case not wearing boots would be a crime against humanity. And she chuckles.

The owner is going full blast, that's one of the drawbacks of this store, and if it weren't for the high quality of footwear they carry it'd be a place to avoid on principle. But there's no real threat, Miranda has a sufficiently clear idea of what she wants, and doesn't let anyone impose. She already has too many dark boots, and she's a bit tired of combining one color with another, basically she always wears the same signature black outfits (so convenient), although she enlivens them with a splash of color or a little jewelry to lighten things up a bit, which is also necessary given her pitch-black hair, which she wears straight and long down over her shoulders. Might they have something a little more colorful? Since she's with Stefania she'd like to benefit from her suggestions, and as she's saying so she flashes her a friendly, complicit smile, the kind of smile Miranda doesn't often give anyone, not even Stefi, while targeting her exact position, down to the inch.

It's odd to hear her use a word like that, thinks Stefi. Colorful, but colorful how? Miranda's been blind from birth so if there's one thing she can neither understand nor even picture it's the concept of color. But the store owner seems even happier to hear that word, and Stefi goes along with it, yes, do show us something a little less classic, but please, no pointy-pointy toes, although she adds that last bit just to get a second smile from Miranda, which, in fact, promptly appears.

Put in this way, their request sounds almost like a challenge. Something less classic? But of course, you could've said so sooner, we'll see right to it, it'll be simple since spring is the best season for going out on a limb, when you're young especially, and girls like them should indulge their desire for change. And she goes on with an entire string of pearls of wisdom, until just a few minutes later Fabiola reappears from the basement with six or seven boxes piled high, meanwhile the owner has kept right on going, telling Miranda and Stefi all about how tough it is to keep up with all the fine leather footwear being made nowadays.

Four of the boots are an immediate no, no, Miranda is unwavering, even though the way she inspects everything with her hands does take a little more time than Stefi had expected and Miranda always wants to hear her opinion of the overall look before making a final decision. So there isn't too much of a selection, and Stefi's favorite is an ankle boot in a subdued maroon, the second ones they brought out, which also comes in two other colors, nothing too edgy, especially if it's paired with the right outfit, a skirt and t-shirt, say, or maybe with jeans, why not? With these even Miranda's lighter jeans would work.

Maroon? Subdued? From the questions fired in her direction Stefi realizes that over the years Miranda has come up with her own highly personal concept of what colors are, because, clearly, coming from her mouth words like bright or subdued and hot or cold are nothing but metaphors taken literally, too literally, as if a given yellow or blue could actually protect you from a harsh climate or cool you off depending on the season, although maybe not like an ice-cold orange juice or a boiling-hot tea, even Miranda must've gathered that much. And so her preference for a fiery red now seems obvious, it sure does lend a lively spark to her otherwise all black ensembles, given the natural temptation to view intensity as a positive thing and subtlety as something lesser, as if pink were a lukewarm form of red and orange were a form of yellow brought back to life, finally starting to flare up into a healthy glow. Maybe that's why, even though Stefi would pick the subdued maroon, Miranda instead goes immediately for a pair of boots with colorful diamonds, its relief pattern permitting her fingers to get a more precise picture, but the three colors must also be a factor, mustard yellow, wine red, and an emeraldy tree-frog green, which is how Stefi described them, trying to be as precise as possible for Miranda's sake, just to be as certain as possible, despite the fact that specifics like these mean nothing whatsoever to her. And yet maybe the description itself was what made the difference, come to think of it that must've been it, because Miranda has tasted mustard and associates it with something a bit spicy, just as she'll have some idea of what emerald green tree frogs are like, such fairytale creatures, and who knows, despite her aggressive comments like tits and ass up for grabs, who's to say she doesn't dream of one day finding her own knight in shining armor, riding into her life astride a white stallion? And why shouldn't she, after all? A knight in shining armor, sure, thinks Stefi, even though the very concept (shining like the springtime sky, shining like the summer sea) implies things she'd find it nearly impossible to comprehend. Totally, they'd go well with black, Stefi says, you just have to pair them with a pretty low-key outfit because otherwise you might look a bit too much like a jester, you know, a bit too carnivalesque, an example that must be pretty clear even to Miranda.

Choosing turns out to be a demanding process. The intensity with which Miranda seems to handle any and every object is endlessly fascinating for Stefi. By now she should be used to it, she's so meticulous, so patient, so completely focused on the feel and consistency of each material whereas Stefania realizes, with a hint of regret, that she's always quite distracted and rushes things. Miranda doesn't always dive into such detailed inspection, generally she's more discreet and doesn't want to stand out any more than she already does, but over the past few months Stefi's happened to surprise her as she's dealing with an unknown object or new space, so she knows how scrupulous Miranda can become in such cases. Even now, even shopping for shoes: there's the outside and the inside, up and down, but above all the stitching of the pattern, the colorful diamonds whose tones Miranda will never really know but whose outlines she can grasp, measuring with her fingertips how much the lines stick out, appreciating the softness of the hand-crafted leather, maybe even fooling herself into thinking that this yellow really does have the spicy flavor of a fine French dijon or that the green is somehow tied to the metaphorical powers possessed by fairytale creatures (while the name wine red will instead likely conjure up the quick tipsiness of alcohol on an empty stomach).

Anyway, even Stefania can feel that the leather is particularly soft, and in the meantime she's begun mirroring Miranda's moves on the twin boot. If you watch Miranda, her precise and minutely attuned gestures but also her concentrated, completely absorbed air, you might get the impression she's touching something special, whereas the boot Stefi's holding strikes her as utterly normal, a boot just like any other, despite the leather's extreme, undeniable softness. She's a bit disappointed. And if she were to try closing her eyes? But that's something Stefi would never do in public, and not only because the downtime has just ended and the saleswoman has started up again with her questions. What do they think? It's from a boutique footwear brand in Vicenza, but they're doing excellent designs and are already making a name for themselves, believe me, boots like this are becoming harder and harder to find nowadays.

Of course they'll round the price down, that's a given. After all, being a regular has its advantages, Stefi thinks, now happy that Miranda liked the store she brought her to, where she and her sister are so familiar and therefore treated so well. It took a while, but the colorful diamond-decorated boots will be simply stunning, Stefi's just sure of it, so sure that she repeats herself two or three times before they turn onto Corso Rinascimento. And yet spring has played a trick on them this year. They realize it just as they're leaving the perfume and body lotion boutique (one of Stefi's old obsessions), you could've guessed that the weather might change but you'd never have predicted a wind like this, they're frozen stiff and now forced to tamp their skirts down with their hands, arms glued to their sides to avoid the unfortunate Marilyn effect, which, if it weren't for the sudden chill in the air, Stefi might even find amusing. At three it was so lovely but now, it's insane, you can never trust the first burst of warmth, thinks Stefi in her short skirt and angora vest atop a matching t-shirt, all so ill-suited to the temperature shifts of this strange April as her entire body begins to tremble, and she wraps herself up in a lightweight designer cardigan, so expensive yet so ineffective against the wind and cold.

Luckily Miranda's place isn't far away, by now her offer of a piping-hot cup of tea couldn't sound any better and Stefi immediately says so, fantastic, she says, fantastic, not just because for a while now Stefi has used this adjective all the time and everything she's experienced over the past few months has, as if by magic, become covered by a coating of fantasy (last fall everything was absurd and insane, which still turn up fairly frequently in her speech, above all when she's a bit tense), nor because it's supremely rare that Stefi ever turns down any of Miranda's ideas. Rather, Stefi's happy that Miranda's finally invited her over to her apartment, her personal den. Seeing someone's place is a decisive, essential step when becoming friends, and come to think of it Stefi doesn't know exactly what to expect in terms of Miranda's apartment, maybe because of the color issue, or because only stupid questions come to mind, like whether there are any lights and how she knows if a bulb is blown, absurd questions like that, which prove that Stefania still can't envision Miranda in a space that's truly her own, or know what to expect, aside from a refuge from the wind, sure, now that protecting herself from the cold suddenly strikes her as the most important thing. Fantastic, Miranda, fantastic.

It's unusual for the weather to take such a sudden turn, although it would sound unforgivably obvious to say anything of the sort. Better keep quiet then, thinks Stefania. So they walk ahead in silence yet swiftly, Miranda shows her the way with a degree of certainty, and all it takes is a turn off Corso Rinascimento for the wind to stop whipping their legs, so the last bit of the way is once again delightful despite the sudden drop in temperature and Stefi again finds her voice: it sounds crazy but they say that false eyelashes are making a comeback. Miranda hasn't even gotten the key into the lock and already Argo starts celebrating her return from the other side of the door, barking, running to and fro, yelping, so different from the responsible and even all-too-calm dog that's usually with her on campus, even with Argo it once again becomes clear that you never really know someone until you see her on her own turf, thinks Stefi, now convinced more than ever that every home holds the soul of its inhabitants, making her even more curious. Then the door opens, finally, and here's super-sweet Argo, he must've missed Miranda and he makes it show, rubbing up against her, sniffing her, nuzzling in with the passion of true love. Rarely has Stefi seen Miranda so happy, as if she's forgotten everything and found peace with life, kneeling down and letting Argo lick her all over, and she responds, equally transported, until Stefi finally admits to herself that maybe Miranda could be happy even without a boyfriend, who's to say otherwise, because everybody's different and Argo must be a huge help, sometimes the love of an animal counts for a lot, a whole lot, despite the fact that without Giorgio, Stefi could never be happy, and the mere thought of having to go on without him makes the cold air outside even colder.

The apartment isn't too large, but it's very tidy. Above all, in spite of Stefi's doubts (insane doubts, pretty embarrassing now), the lights all seem to be in working order and Miranda never forgets to turn them on before bringing her into the room. We blind people really have to be organized, she points out right off the bat (it's odd that Miranda never uses the term visually impaired, Stefi can't help but notice every time, even if a slight crudeness somehow suits Miranda's style as a strong and independent woman, which is, after all, her defining trait). It's a matter of survival, she goes on, but today you're especially in luck, the cleaning lady came this morning, so just keep in mind that I can't take any credit for anything that's spotless, shiny, or freshly scented in this house.

Stefi is particularly struck by the large white library, especially because a book collection like this is the last thing you'd expect to see at Miranda's place. She's clearly not the first person to react this way because as soon as she says wow, so many books, with a tone of admiration, Miranda's all too quick to reply, a lot of them are braille but most of them are audiobooks or radio recordings on CD and cassette, the shelves continue into the hallway and bedroom, where I keep my music, and last time I counted there were over four thousand CDs alone. But Stefi already knows the rest of the story. When they found out their daughter was blind, meaning visually impaired (Stefi simply must silently correct Miranda on that, every time), Miranda's parents focused on her education, her father's business was going well and so her mother had retired early from teaching in order to concentrate on her daughter's music and language skills, she said it was to help make up for her handicap, and that's why Miranda speaks such perfect French and English, ever since she was little she was always looked after by a native speaker, so you can just imagine what an effort that was, hon. But don't be fooled, Miranda continues, aside from the classical music CDs it's all appearances, braille books take up double or triple the amount of space normal books do, and a specialized institute up in Monza sends them upon request, for free: all you have to do is ask. *War and Peace,* for example, is right behind you, and it alone takes up two-thirds of the shelf, so just do the math.

That must be the book Miranda's hand is gently touching, even if from the outside and with no visible title Stefi has no way of knowing.

No writing, no photos, which wouldn't do Miranda any good anyway, so different from the books she's used to dealing with. May I have a look? She asks, and Miranda answers right away, Go ahead, in the meantime, what can I get you? Shall I brew some tea, or would you like something a little stronger? as she heads for the kitchen. Tea would be great: for warming up, Stefi says, there's nothing like a cup of piping-hot tea.

Actually, all you have to do is hunt for it, on closer inspection the title and author are there on the spine (yup, Tolstoy, and sure enough it's *War and Peace*), along with the address of the institute up in Monza: that, too, reassures her. But, rather than a book, it seems more like a poorly bound dissertation done at the local copy shop, like the ones Stefi's seen so many of around campus, the same oversize page formats (in this case they're more square than rectangular), the same colorful spiral bindings, if it weren't for the different paper stock, so thick, rigid, and heavy, in a particularly dull, light-absorbing shade of white. In these new trappings, Tolstoy looks even more menacing. How many volumes could there be? This is volume six, but it doesn't seem like the last, even though the writing covers both sides of the page and the trim size is more like an atlas than a nineteenth-century classic. Seven? Eight? Nine? Maybe for now it's best to check whether Miranda needs her help with the tea.

Even in the kitchen rounded forms reign supreme (oval-shaped table, curved countertop). In Miranda's house there's a ban on all angles, by avoiding sharp corners you can spare yourself a whole lot of bruises, and Stefi's heard it said that this is a fairly common precaution taken in homes of the visually impaired. Pretty genius. And Miranda doesn't even seem to need it, to judge by the fluidity of her moves as soon as she's in a familiar space. It's insane, Stefi's never seen her this way, and as she watches her fill the teapot and turn on the stove's middle burner Stefi can't help but admire Miranda's agility as she pops from one drawer to the next, fridge, dishrack, chopping-block chest, it seems she can see, she's suddenly freed of the caution that usually accompanies each and every gesture when she's out and about on the street or on campus. Teacups and spoons, sugar and sweetener, and a fine selection of teas have appeared out of nowhere, in a flash, and Miranda guides her through them as they wait for the water to boil. Darjeeling or Earl Grey? Or, if it won't keep her up, there's a bit of superb Irish breakfast left, a friend brought it over a few months ago from England: this is a Miranda she's never seen before.

May I use the bathroom? Stefi suddenly asks. Miranda points to the door at the end of the hallway, on the left, that's the one, the apartment is small so you can't miss it. And Stefi doesn't miss it. The ocean green and bright cerulean colors (tiny tiles, undoubtely more elegant than most) are rather common, although she really likes the large mirror and terrycloth robe, which is super-soft (you could've guessed as much). And the hydromassage showerhead inspires envy, too. That's the first thing Stefi checks on because she's been asking for one for years with no luck, despite her best efforts she's never managed to persuade her parents to have one installed and the moment you mention the idea of bringing workmen into the house her mother protests, but only when it's something Stefi wants. It's so clear by now, by now she knows, because whenever it was something else, like installing lights on the patio, her mother had no complaints,with the pretext that the work was out in the garden. The marble sink is pretty nice too, so large, with a lot of countertop room to keep the most frequently used products in plain sight, and for Miranda that must really be convenient, because in her condition searching for anything can become an immense undertaking if you don't have anyone there to ask for help. Denman hairbrushes are the best to avoid irritating the scalp, nice choice, and then there are various combs and a whole set of creams, it doesn't seem like Miranda has very sensitive skin, not as sensitive as Stefi's at least, but with such a wide variety it's clear that even she pays great attention to it. The perfumes, on the other hand, are in the cabinet off to the right, complete with clever little dividers inside to keep bottles from falling over as you search for just the right one, both clever and useful (in Miranda's case more than ever). Chanel and Armani, in this department Miranda has fairly traditional tastes, just as Stefi figured. Medicines are lower down, vitamins, aspirin, ibuprofen (Stefi takes it for menstrual cramps, Miranda, well, who knows?), small stuff, Relpax (Stefi had no idea Miranda suffered from migraine), sleeping pills, ah-ha, as I was saying, that's bad, a really bad sign, something's amiss here. And the other cabinet? Stefi would gladly take a peek, only because she wants to be close, closer (of course), with Miranda everything's always so difficult, Miranda so rarely opens up, as if her visually impaired condition weren't already enough to complicate things between them. Now, though, she'd best get back, the tea must be ready and if Stefania keeps on dawdling Miranda might get worried. So she flushes the toilet and a second later joins her on the large white sofa.

Over tea Stefi goes back to talking about Miranda's library: it's insane, another one of those things she'd never have imagined, like Miranda's fashion sense and all those hi-tech gadgets on her computer. And so, flipping through the book that seems to be *War and Peace*, Stefania wonders what it's like to read braille, yeah, there's yet another thing about Miranda she'll never get to know. Sometimes she feels like no matter how much of an effort she makes, there's always an impenetrable barrier between them, no matter how hard she tries, Stefi's doomed to remain an outsider, just like Miranda will only be able to imagine the colors of her new boots without ever really grasping what mustard yellow or wine red are despite the infinite associations those resonant names conjure up by analogy, and that always gets her down.

Would you like to try? Miranda asks just then, suddenly and yet somehow on cue, as if she could read her mind. Weird: that's just how Miranda is, psychic and intuitive, that must be the word, psychic (or intuitive), because sometimes Stefi finds the way Miranda picks up on things is a bit supernatural (sometimes), like for example when Miranda seems to know where Stefania is in the classroom even if she hasn't uttered a single word. But more than anything Stefi's happy that Miranda's now trying to make her a part of her world, something Miranda never does, which has always made her sorry. Of course she'd like to, but how? And so Miranda grabs none other than *War and Peace*, which is right within reach and which Stefi, to her great shame, has never read, too long, too long even for Stefi who's reputed to be an avid reader, but she doesn't fess up to Miranda and so now, in braille, stretching across a half-yard of shelf space, Tolstoy makes her feel even more uneasy than before. Opening it to a random page, she invites her to touch it, running her fingertips across the tiny bumps. Like this? Like that. Exactly. Miranda guides her, tries teaching her to recognize the letters one by one, a, b, c, the general principles are simple but as soon as she tries decoding entire words the signs are all jumbled up again and after ten minutes Stefi feels like she hasn't made even the slightest progress, even though she can recognize some characters with her eyes, her fingers can't tell the difference, the characters are all the same, so much the same that she almost immediately gives up trying and merely pretends to be really interested, mechanically repeating a sequence of uh-huhs and yups just to be nice, basically she's distracted but makes like she's perpetually on the brink of mastering the braille alphabet. If only . . .

Luckily the tea interrupts them: tea is to be enjoyed before it cools off, Miranda reminds her, always the perfect hostess. They sip it in silence and Stefi's happy that her experimentation with braille is over, it's better this way, even if she feels her fumbled tries created an atmosphere of complicity that's pretty rare with Miranda. Maybe it's the apartment, or the afternoon spent together, or her awkward attempts at getting the hang of that strange system, but for once it seems Miranda's stopped being so defensive (Miranda, who she's starting to become friends with). And that's why Miranda's next question doesn't catch her off guard, wanting to touch her face, feel what she looks like. She thinks she's heard it's fairly common that the blind ask things like that of their friends and so she was expecting it sooner or later, or at least that's what Stefi seems to think she knows now, probably from films and novels, because now she can't really recall but even without recalling Miranda's request doesn't sound so unusual. To touch her face, feel what she looks like: of course. Naturally this doesn't mean that Stefi's calm or doesn't find it a little disquieting, not at all, quite the contrary, because right about now Stefi's anything but. Where has she seen a scene like this before? At the movies, definitely, or maybe on TV (she thinks), there's no real difference, also because the only thing that comes to mind now is *Ghost*, how romantic, such a tear-jerker back when she was a teen, especially that scene where Demi Moore, thanks to the powers of psychic medium Whoopi Goldberg, gets to touch the face of her dead husband Patrick Swayze, who's dead and has become a ghost, but still isn't ready to leave her behind and does everything he can to protect her, even from the beyond. Oh, so romantic. This won't exactly be the same thing, but right now that's the only example Stefi can recall, since between the ages of twelve and sixteen she must've watched that tape at least ten times with her best friend at the time, Sara, who she then discovered was an ungrateful, totally fake friend (but only later). So because of all that she simply replies no, she wouldn't mind at all, really, no problem, Miranda. And she closes her eyes, waiting, sinking into the sofa with the same sense of resignation with which she'd surrender to having a molar pulled, all resistance already worn down yet already anxious, now that even the white of the room makes her think of a dental office. What a wuss.

By surprise, Miranda begins with her forehead. It's strange because if Stefi had to describe her gestures she'd say first and foremost that Miranda lingers on the least expected areas of her face, disregarding for example her nose, which for Stefi has always been her number-one point of pride, the French nose inherited from her mother, pretty and pointing somewhat upward, although Stefi's is actually a little longer and just a tiny bit pointier, more foxlike (from her daddy), a barely detectable difference that Giorgio says makes her even more attractive because it activates her face's many contours, whatever he might mean by that. Instead, it's as if Miranda were tracing her face's boundaries, first her ears and then moving downward, cheekbones, cheeks, and finally chin, running both hands down to either side, as if to get a full image of the outer oval, a complete idea of it, before bringing her hands toward the center (but still no nose). Why doesn't she try to relax a bit? It'd be so much better. Though unfortunately Stefi remains knotted up tight. It's an odd feeling, we're not used to letting anyone touch our face, not like this (not like this), even with beauty-spa masks and massages there's no comparison, it's too different, this could even be enjoyable if Stefi could only manage to lie back and loosen up a bit. Impossible. At times Miranda hesitates a moment, on her eyelids, or on her lips (dried out and cracked, just like her throat, totally dry despite the tea), and each time it seems to Stefi as if Miranda has discovered something even she doesn't know about, something wrong, definitely (even if she couldn't say what), something she'd like to ask Miranda about right away, what've you found? What is it, c'mon just tell me. It's tempting but Stefi keeps her mouth shut and her eyes closed tight, just like when Giorgio kisses her, meaning there's no real reason she doesn't open her eyes and look at Miranda as she studies her contours but instead keeps them closed just the same. Why has she paused again? Each time the scene repeats and Miranda stops, Stefi's anxiety grows once more, she's rooting about, rummaging around, it's as if Miranda were peering inside her, reading Stefi's mind with her hands, and it wouldn't be the first time Stefi's had to surrender to Miranda's sixth sense and surprising psychic abilities.

May I? Miranda then asks, hesitating on the edge of Stefi's neck, and she has no idea how to answer. Can she? Can she not? And can she what, exactly? Stefi hesitates but then, just the same, replies yes, sure, even if Stefi isn't at all sure, but that doesn't matter because Miranda has her own special way of destabilizing Stefi and in the end that's a good thing, Giorgio's right (in the end), Stefi's always been too sheltered if such a simple, everyday question can launch her into such an agitated state, a question from a friend who only wants to get to know her a bit better so they can be even better friends afterward. But above all Stefi doesn't want to offend Miranda and would be sorry if she were to sense her embarrassment, Stefi's gotta quit being so upset since there's nothing wrong, nothing uncomfortable about Miranda's fingertips running along her neck and heading for her breasts but turning just before and immediately going back upward only to plunge downward once again with renewed intent, lower down, back toward her breasts. But it only lasts a moment. Miranda is delicate and, considering the way she follows the curve of Stefi's neck, discreet, even, discreet in her indiscretion is the way Stefi comes to think of it, and now feels a bit confused and continues repeating to herself that the blind have their own way of communicating, Stefi knows that much, it's a whole other language, with other limits, other boundaries, and at least now she's stopped feeling like she's under investigation the way she did when

Miranda was touching her face and seemed to be reading Stefi's mind through her fingertips. It isn't unpleasant and Stefi should try getting over this anxiety, relaxing like when she goes for a massage, because Miranda really is quite delicate and is just barely touching her, almost a caress but not even, to call it a caress would be too much, and all it would take is for Stefi to truly convince herself that Miranda's hands are her eyes to then get past the obstacle of this sudden intimacy. Stefi really tries, although at this point there isn't a thought in the world that could possibly relieve the tension triggered by those fingers touching her with a gentleness so unlike Giorgio's, even when Giorgio wants and knows how to be gentle, except that it is Giorgio and couldn't be anyone but Giorgio because only he is allowed to touch her so freely, without asking and yet asking and receiving, even if his way is different and even if this way isn't the same but something pretty close to it, too close to it, thinks Stefi as she continues keeping her eyes closed, telling herself once again that they aren't those hands just like they aren't those fingertips, which Stefi has learned to recognize, because it doesn't strike her as right that Miranda should touch her as only Giorgio does and so then what counts is that it's different, so then all she needs to do is remember that Miranda is blind and this is just Miranda's way of seeing her.

And suddenly Stefania is hot, unbearably hot. A sticky and awkward hot. This is yet another reason she'd like to move, but Miranda picks up on her discomfort and pauses.

"Does that tickle?" she asks, almost considerately.

"No," replies Stefi with an almost normal voice, more steady than she herself had expected. "I'm just a bit warm. It must be all the tea we drank."

"Do you want to take off your sweater?"

"No, that isn't necessary. But if you don't mind I'll go get a glass of cold water. You want anything?"

Afterward, on the sofa once again, and without the sweater, things are already better: along with the heat the embarrassment she felt just a moment ago has also disappeared, both have vanished, just like that. Indeed, precisely because Stefi feels safer and Miranda's so quiet, Stefi feels the need to say something, anything, and even if no one has asked she's compelled to comment on what's happened, so she starts babbling on about their friendship and how friendship means being able to put yourself in other people's shoes. She really liked trying to read braille, for example, because now she feels like she has a better understanding of Miranda's world (this is just another little lie and Stefi can't stifle the slight and involuntary smile that briefly curls her lips upward but it doesn't matter since Miranda won't be able to see anyway). You know, Stefania continues, earlier, when you were touching my face, I felt like you were peering deep inside of me, nothing like that has ever happened to me before, it was as if you could read my mind, especially when you focused on a single spot. Isn't that absurd?

"Who says I wasn't?" Miranda forcefully replies. "You can't even imagine how many things I found out about you." She laughs, as does Stefania, close behind.

Only then does Miranda ask her if she'd like to try, too. At first Stefi doesn't understand. Meaning . . ? Meaning switch places, with Stefania touching Miranda's face exactly the way Miranda had touched Stefania's face earlier, and if she's good at it she'll be able to read her mind, too. But she shouldn't get her hopes up: that takes practice and perseverance, even if Miranda admits she might have a bit of beginner's luck and find out who-knows-what about her, it's unlikely but you never know (another laugh). Well then?

As a matter of principle Stefania never goes against anything Miranda says, but as soon as Miranda begins blindfolding her her heart starts racing like mad. Too tight? No, that's perfect. At first Stefi didn't really understand why the scarf was so necessary, but now she sees Miranda was right about habit (obviously), all-powerful habit, opening her eyes would ruin the whole thing and then so much for their experiment (so much for reciprocity). In light of all that it's obvious and even necessary that the scarf come into play. That's fine but don't pull it any tighter. C'mon, I already told you I can't see a thing.

Well then, here we are. Here? Here. Stefi certainly isn't at ease, there's no use hiding, it's awkward, she's awkward and clumsy but doesn't waste any time, so she runs her fingers over Miranda's nose and cheeks, at first she worries about hurting her, maybe scratching Miranda by accident with her long nails, or she worries about the opposite, about not feeling anything and having to fake it, like with Tolstoy and those damned braille characters that to her touch really all felt the same. But no. Stefi immediately realizes that no special practice is required to recognize eyebrows and lips, earlobes, you know, or the little indentation below the nose she discovers she doesn't know the name of, while this is a lock of hair stuck to her forehead, definitely, Miranda's slightly sweaty forehead thanks to the tea they drank together. What's more, it isn't true that Miranda's skin isn't sensitive. Stefi was wrong, so wrong, Miranda's skin now seems so soft to the touch, especially on her cheeks and neck, because Stefi doesn't know where to stop but has resolved to stick to the face, now moving both hands symmetrically, on both right and left, slowly moving upward, just the way she felt Miranda do it, right and left simultaneously, to outline little by little the oval of her face, even if Stefania, of course, already knows Miranda's face. She tries to guess what it would be like to reconstruct what Miranda looks like using only her hands but it's impossible, even if Stefi can't see right now her visual memory of Miranda always gains the upper hand, recalibrating everything, for example her unexpectedly soft, smooth skin and her eyebrows, perfectly plucked. Miranda, too, keeps her eyes closed and Stefi can touch her eyelids, it's odd to feel the eyeballs moving underneath (moving almost imperceptibly, how odd). Because it's from details like this, above all, that Stefi really comes to understand that she's touching a living thing, or from her breath, because Miranda's now breathing with her mouth slightly open.

"Everything okay?"

"Yeah, everything's fine," Stefi replies, even if she feels like she should be the one asking Miranda, especially since she's worried she'll accidentally scratch her with her long nails.

"How 'bout you, my nails aren't scratching?"

"All right. I'm all right, too."

Now she's a bit calmer, because even though it's true Stefi's a real wuss, it's also true that it takes very little to reassure her. She returns to Miranda's nose, chin, and lips, just like before (always watching out for her nails, which are so long, and might scratch her), forehead and ears, exactly like before, until suddenly Stefi senses something, an unexpected movement, she can't see but she can clearly intuit (or rather feel, that is she thinks she feels) that Miranda's shifting position, as if to lean toward her, no longer sinking back into the sofa but leaning forward, almost mirroring Stefi's stance, more upright and closer up, leaving Stefi unsure whether to go on or stop, also because she's breathing deeply and her heart is pumping full throttle just like every time she's taken by surprise. What's going on? Stefi can't see Miranda but senses that soon she'll be on top of her or at least that's what she's thinking in the heat of the moment, she can almost feel Miranda's breath on her face, Miranda's lips too close to her lips, and suddenly she's sure of it or it's as if she were sure, do something, do something now, because Stefi can't see but it's as if she could because she's so sure (even though Miranda hasn't touched her yet), so it's just instinctual and without thinking that she holds her hands up to push Miranda away before it's too late and yells no, Miranda, no, Stefi doesn't even know why she's shouting so loud but it's a shout (it's a shout all right), pushing her away with a violence that stuns her before it does anyone else. Leave me, I told you to leave me alone!

But Miranda doesn't say a thing nor does she try to hold her back, as Stefi would've expected. No battle, no resistance. It's better this way. She's free, now Stefania is free and has shed the blindfold, as she continues repeating that everything's all right and nothing happened at all (don't worry, Stefi, everything's fine: as if that were all it took). Because suddenly Stefania is embarrassed and would like to say something, now that she's opened her eyes she realizes how melodramatic her gesture was, as soon as she lost her sight she lost control, all control, it's clear (shouting like that, for example: totally absurd), even if Miranda, well, Stefi couldn't have dreamt it, it's crazy but true, Miranda was about to—or not? Yup, absolutely, it's unbelievable, she was about to. Miranda of all people. Stefi doesn't finish her thought, but there's no need, it's so obvious, her Miranda . . . How insane. Now what? More than anything Stefi would like another glass of water, but she doesn't dare make a move. Miranda, on the other hand, has little by little slid toward the opposite side of the sofa, far from Stefi and motionless, she doesn't say a thing and if the expression were capable of meaning anything in her case you'd even say she refuses to look at Stefi (but in Miranda's case that expression makes no sense).

Suddenly everything's so absurd, so totally absurd, and now the room actually does resemble a doctor's office. And as if that weren't enough, there's the time, almost eight, if Stefi wants to go home to at least grab a jacket she has to go now, even if she gets a cab, from here to Parioli isn't exactly around the corner, and she certainly can't face the evening dressed so lightly, with only a jersey, but now even just running up doesn't seem like an option. And that's assuming you even find a cab: available cabs are few and far between on Friday nights. But then again even thinking of dinner feels out of place right now. She's made a mess of things, that's for sure. Miranda was about to—uh-huh, there's no doubt, at least for Stefi there isn't the slightest shadow of a doubt, almost definitely. What a mess. Now she won't want to see her anymore: well, you know, meet up (Stefi's beginning to get fed up with all these sight-based expressions). If only Giorgio weren't so obsessed with people being on time! But even Stefi knows it's only an excuse. Who'd ever have thought? Miranda.

Stefi doesn't move, Miranda doesn't speak. Three past eight. Four past eight. It's all so insane. Five past eight. Anything, anything just to break the tension:

"Look, Miranda, I have to go."

Silence. Since Miranda doesn't say a word, Stefi tries to speak, now she has no idea what came over her and she's once again afraid she's ruined everything:

"Miranda, don't take this the wrong way, I . . ."

"Don't worry about it, Stefania. Go."

Stefania, not Stefi. Miranda's back to her old self, tough, defensive, basically the Miranda everybody knows, the one that's once again starting to frighten her a bit. The next sentence stings even more:

"Thanks for helping me go shoe shopping." Stefi comes back:

"No, really, it's just that I have to go . . ."

"I get it, you have to go. No problem. Thanks for the afternoon."

"Okay, but I just want you to . . . understand . . . what I mean is, don't get the wrong idea . . . You know Giorgio's expecting me. We have a dinner."

"Go ahead, it's okay. Don't worry about it."

It's okay, don't worry. But that's not what the tone of her voice is saying, the tremendous seriousness of Miranda's voice all of a sudden makes her feel even worse. Indeed, Stefi doesn't budge, she doesn't have the strength and so she at least tries to speak, to repeat that she has to go in hopes that the words will give her the courage she needs to get up off the sofa:

"I'm going, then."

"Look, I've got it: you've been saying that over and over for five minutes now. Go ahead. You can see, so you shouldn't have any trouble finding the way out. I trust you'll excuse me for not showing you to the door."

"Please, Miranda, don't do that."

"I'm not doing a damn thing. Goodbye."

"I'm going but I'll call. I'll call you tomorrow, I promise."

"Don't bother. I don't need your charity."

"I swear I'll call, but I hope you can forgive me. Oh, please, Miranda. I . . . I'll call you after dinner if we're not out too late. I have to go now but I'll totally call you. Later. But don't turn your phone off."

"Goodbye, Stefania."

"Bye . . . Bye ."

Out on the street, Stefi's still a little stunned. All of a sudden, just now, she realizes Miranda's scarf is in her hand. She put her sweater and vest back on gripping it in her fist, and now she looks at it bewildered, she doesn't know what to do with it, until she puts it in her pocket: to give it back the next chance she gets, she thinks, but only partly believes it. Stefi looks at the time: twelve past eight, already, she can't even dream of stopping by home now, nor can she stay out in the cold, the temperature has dropped even farther and Stefi's way underdressed. If only there were a store open she could just stop in and buy something, but it's too late already, everything's closed. What a day. At least a cab, a cab straightaway, so long as she doesn't have to wait in this harsh cold for a cab to show up at the stand on Via Zanardelli. But there's no line and . . . voilà, she's in luck. This is what you call luck. I'm going to Duke's, she says, on Viale Parioli, you know the place?

Once she's inside things are better. So Stefi even gets there early, and while she's paying for the ride she starts wondering whether maybe she should've tried stopping by home, just to grab something a bit warmer. Eight-thirty on the dot, from Via Zanardelli to Viale Parioli in eighteen minutes, almost a record. And on Friday: even more insane. But above all a full fifteen minutes to freshen up a bit before Giorgio and the others arrive. But the bar's too crowded, Stefi just hopes no one approaches her, not tonight, not now, someone sitting by herself at a place like this during happy hour means there's almost a mathematical certainty that within five minutes someone will walk up and start talking her ear off, a young woman by herself at Duke's at eight thirty, it seems obvious, but Stefi has no desire to defend herself, not today at least, as if what she's already been through weren't enough.

"What can I get you?" the waitress asks a little too promptly, and Stefi, who usually doesn't like strong drinks but hasn't had time to look at the list, ends up ordering a glass of port. How odd. But port is sweet and it does her good, she's never tried it on an empty stomach before, the alcohol goes straight to her head, which isn't unpleasant after the kind of afternoon she's just left behind. The minutes pass and Stefi calms down (thanks to the port, for sure), and most importantly nobody walks up to her, which is totally new. She must really look shaken if nobody tries to chat her up, she thinks: at Duke's, and at this hour. Giorgio absolutely mustn't see her in this state, but luckily Stefi has everything she needs in her handbag, all it'll take is not even two minutes in the ladies' room and she'll come back a new woman, for Giorgio and for their friends.

Sure enough, with her face freshly washed and a quick touch-up to her makeup, Stefi already feels a bit better. Eight forty-three: it's almost time. At first she plays around with her phone to give the impression she's waiting for a call and to dissuade potential flirts, a trick she learned from Lavinia, like constantly looking at your watch even if you don't need to know the time. But in reality Stefi keeps pulling up Miranda's number in her contacts, just because, completely by chance, since it's one of the last numbers she called and to better fend off the guys at the bar. Did she imagine it all? That's something Stefi doesn't even want to consider. She felt, that is, she believed she felt . . . Now she's no longer so certain, and that would really be terrible (because now she's no longer so certain). She'd like to call her but doesn't know, she even begins writing a text message or two, only to give up, it isn't easy to find the right words, especially when you imagine Miranda's going to listen to them being read by that impersonal voice that converts them into voicemails. Miranda. Who'd have thought (really, who'd ever have thought)? And Stefi was so worried to see her without a boyfriend. But now her reaction has ruined everything, absolutely everything. She writes then deletes, then starts writing again and then deletes again, until the last few minutes pass and Giorgio shows up at the door, eight forty-five, punctual as always when he has a date. He sees her and comes over, he's in a great mood, happy that she's on time for once, and greets her with a kiss on the neck, an impassioned kiss that gives her a start, asking her how the afternoon went, you know, the long-awaited shopping date with Batgirl. This time Stefi doesn't respond, but thinks: Batgirl, here we go again. Then she says, calmly: "Really well. We didn't find anything, unfortunately. I'll tell you about it later, it isn't easy, you know, in her condition. So I had to promise I'd go with her again next weekend."

But Giorgio's no longer listening to her, he's getting up to go meet Ludovico and Arianna, who've just entered the bar (Arianna with super-short, surprisingly ash-blonde hair, Ludovico in a blue suit that shows how well his new diet is going). Too bad. If only he'd look at Stefi he'd notice a sudden contraction of her lips, almost like the start of the involuntary smiles he knows so well by now, but this time it effortlessly morphs into a warm welcome for their friends, for Arianna and for Ludovico who, perfectly on time, are strolling forward through the tables at Duke's and starting to wave. ■

Translated by Alta L. Price

Franca Di Muzio lives on the Adriatic coast of Italy in Pescara (Abruzzi), where she received her honors degree in foreign languages and literature, majoring in English and Russian. She works as a copywriter, editor, and journalist, but has also taken time in finding her own voice, by writing the screenplay *United Colors* (IXth Biennial of Young Artists from Europe and the Mediterranean) and by publishing a number of short stories (most of which have English titles) in anthologies and magazines: "Disabled Goggles" (*Sagarana*), "Defensor" (Fernandel Editore), "Happy Feet" (Perrone Editore), "Hairquake" (*Sagarana*), "Oblivion" ("Montesilvano scrive" writing contest), "Nunzio Show" (Galaad Edizioni), and "The Rat Race" (Ibis Edizioni). Among her works with Italian titles, the short story "Sorvegliato Speciale" (in the magazine *Abbiamo le prove*) and the novel *Lo scopriremo solo scrivendo* (shortlisted for the Calvino Prize) are worth mentioning.

The following short story was originally published with the title "Alzati e cammina" in the literary magazine *Fernandel*, April 2010, and was awarded the Teramo Prize for best short story in 2010.

ARISE AND WALK

Franca Di Muzio

The next time you hear of a miracle, take notice of the day on which it happened. Which day of the week, just saying. Take notice, then tell me whether it's a Saturday or a Sunday, when we work killing ourselves before resting, relaxing, having fun in order to escape the harassing questions about the meaning of the life we lead on working days; when each event acquires a special light, or shadow.

Take Lazarus. We do not know exactly on which day he was resurrected, but I'd bet my new dolly shoes on a Sunday, after a string of mournful hours punctuated by the wailing of his sisters had finally talked Jesus into the need of making an exception to human rules, by snatching him from the world of the dead.

The man born blind, on the other hand, should certainly have had his sight restored on a Saturday, the day devoted to forced rest, benefiting from the spirit of contradiction of the One who came not to unite but to divide, to separate sons from fathers, daughters from mothers, wheat from chaff, et cetera.

And the mysterious, disturbing haemorrhagic woman? She most likely stopped bleeding on a Sunday; just in time to recharge and with renewed, submissive female spirit, set to deal with the domestic labors of the week to come.

If, therefore, it had to happen, it could only be on a Saturday or a Sunday, preferably in the late afternoon, while the sun evaporates behind the mountains of the Fara. We would have been petrified in the dark, stunned, incredulous, fraternized forever by an ineffable moment crumbling into tears, screams, hugs, prayer beads, booze, laughter, singing, dancing, conversions, confessions. At dawn, the news would roll down the valley, sudden like an avalanche, attracting television channels and reportages, excommunications and blessings, difficult routes up and down the mountains' tortuous bends, curious throngs besieging the old woman's house.

* * *

I don't remember exactly how it began. At a certain point, in a certain point of the Apennines, something had happened to someone; something which had disrupted the common course of things, making us think about the unthinkable: a miracle. Somehow, the good news had landed on the Adriatic coast, not too far from our neighborhood; and in a market, a square or churchyard someone had heard it, and told it to someone else, who had referred it to some neighbor, who in turn had spoken it to Angela's family. From there, from listening to those hopeful words, our little caravan hadn't taken long to start and leave. Walking all the way to the happy, incredible moment where Angela would have finally walked.

* * *

The old woman would "put her hands" only on the weekends. By the mid of the week, our families would get together, to discuss whether it was better to go on a Saturday (in case the following day someone had to attend a baptism or communion) or, rather, on a Sunday, taking advantage of reduced traffic along the way. Be that as it may, we had to leave early in the morning, when there was enough daylight: Fara being so far away, and with all those winding curves!

Gassed up, control the water and oil levels, a minimum of supplies, a tip to the old woman: we performed our propitiatory rites with the zeal of somebody who has discovered or rediscovered something, someone to trust, shooting ahead toward the departure.

The first to move were the fathers. Right after lunch, they would give up their sacred naps and go down into the garages to awaken their Prinz, Simca, Fiat 127 and Fiat 850, stripping away their waxed silver covers, opening the garage doors with large and vigorous gestures. While their engines warmed up, our mothers had plenty of time to wrap us up and load us on board, along with an exaggerated amount of rosaries, sandwiches and oranges.

We would arrive right on time for the meeting, scheduled in the tiny square in front of Angela's place. Our neighbors, hidden behind their windows, would look at our line of cars, some of them addressing us with a short greeting or blessing, others disbelievingly shaking their heads. Deep down, who knows, perhaps they envied us, and would have liked to join us if only they had believed enough. Who knows if we were better than them, or if we were just some poor, deluded people? I wondered if we really had faith, if I had it! Who knows what I hoped for, what I believed, what I was supposed to do there, squeezed in the back seat of a car, a little girl's salami in a sandwich of mothers, looking at an indefinite point on the glass of the car's window, lost in the effort to visualize my best friend standing up, her bulk of atrophied muscles suddenly animated by a divine spark. Would she feel pain? Would she scream, cry or smile? Or all three at once? I strived every time to imagine the scene, but I could not see it. For indeed, miracles are like this: something incredible, something never seen before. Something happening somewhere, somewhere between the course of ages . . . who knows, maybe next weekend.

* * *

The next time would be the right one. At age eleven, Angela would still have time to play, jump, go to discos, rub up to a boy, doing all those things that, sooner or later, befell all girls, even the ugliest ones. Within the time of an exciting weekend, she would discover and memorize in her faculties the ease of motion verbs. Modern dancing, swimming, tennis, hiking in the mountains: she would join all those courses; attend them all at the same time.

Through the fury of moving, she would shed that weird, lopsided belly of hers, and every guy would have fallen in love with her. She would have invaded the entire neighborhood with her smile, coupling it with a very short skirt, a magnet attracting dirty, sensuous words. She would be the first to be invited to all parties, forever. She would have immediately forgotten me, about the fifteen minutes it took me to warm her frozen fingers as we walked to school, to remove her coat in the classroom by gently flexing her inert arms, to open her schoolbag, pulling out notebooks, snacks, books, her diary in which I used to write down her homework whenever she got tired of writing. Those afternoons we used to spend closed in her house studying and playing, except that time: it had snowed more than a foot and a half and I had ran out with the other kids of the building, entranced and frenzied, throwing bullet-like snowballs at each other, making a Babelic snowman. While I was inserting a carrot-nose on its face, my mom called me back home with a precise order: take this pot, stuff it with some of that soft, frosty whiteness and take it immediately to Angela.

The next time on the Fara mountains, the pain she had endured during the first eleven years of her life would melt faster than that snow, like cold, dirty water which one would throw down the sink without a thought. She would become whole and happy, Angela; able to go out at last, to make and throw her own snowballs, to feel the muscles of her lower back tensing up while going down toward the pavement to adjust the bow of her new, shiny dolly shoes.

I stared at my own shoes, their red, satanic glow looming at me from the pavement. I enjoyed moving their heels and toes up and down, trying to catch some ray of light so as to make them sparkle more. I don't know if I really wished a miracle to happen. And I wasn't the only one.

* * *

In the happy possibility of a healthy future for Angela, our parish priest wouldn't believe. Like heck we told him about the holy pictures, statues and madonnas hanging in the old woman's house, where we did nothing else but pray, and where somebody else had already had their miracle: "That's Satan's meal!" he would hiss every Sunday morning from a historiated pulpit, staring down at us in his special way of making us feel uneasy, incomplete and guilty even if we hadn't done anything wrong. Guilty of hoping, of having faith in the impossible. Shouldn't he encourage us? After all, it was him who kept telling us about Lazarus, about the man born blind, about the haemorrhagic woman, Ask and You Shall Receive, Go, Your Faith Has Saved Thee? But the Reverend seemed to believe only in dead and buried miracles, the ones made with loaves and fish long ago digested, with water and wine which had dried up ages ago. Only there one could find the true Jesus Christ; while the rest was Satan's meal.

When the Reverend came up with this story of Satan's meal, he gave me the creeps. Because up in Fara there was, in fact, a large mill: the largest in Italy, renowned even abroad, hailed by advertising. A behemoth, employing hundreds of people, belching flour and pasta that would reach all the kitchen tables of the world, from the most humble to the most prestigious. From things so good nothing wrong could come, I reassured myself; that's why next time I'd get in the car again, enduring Fara's bending curves and the pressure of our mother's elbows on my sides, until I would, again, find myself in front of that door, jumping from one dolly shoe to another.

* * *

Every time she would open the door in an annoyed, distracted fashion, as if she hadn't been waiting for us, as if she had been too busy stirring some kind of concoction requiring mandatory cooking times that our presence would have irreparably compromised. A wooden rosary, polished from use, knotted up around her gnarled hands; that distant expression on her face, typical of people born and raised in the mountains, accustomed to heights. An expression that our city mothers feared: they would murmur their greetings while the old woman would only slightly move aside just a little, barely enough to let them pass, one at a time, while keeping her stare fixed on them while they'd pile up their bags and coats on her one and only filthy couch.

She seemed not take notice of me; besides, her focus was all on Angela, who was being pushed in her wheelchair toward the center of a rotten dining room with a sort of anticipatory enthusiasm which would be more pronounced every time. Once settled in, Angela's face would invariably become red, possibly from the cold mountain air or from the embarrassment of being there, surrounded by chairs, moms and rosaries, bearing the weight of collective hope. Yet, she must have already been accustomed to people's attention, to their pitiful stares, their improper questions: at age eleven, she had already built her own emotional boomerang, made up of cold glances and bright smiles with which she would shoot back straight into people's faces their unwanted pity. But within those stale walls, dominated by the imperious stare of the old woman, her vulnerability would surface at last, masked by hope and faith in the impossible feat of defeating the monster that lived in her body from birth, to extending the relentless thirty-year expiration date of her life.

* * *

"Nobody and nothing can resist the powers of the Rosary and Our Lady. Not even the devil, nor evil, nor disease. Ask, and you shall receive. You just have to pray, have faith, everyone! Angela will walk again."

Ave Maria Gratia Plena Dominus Tecum Et Benedictus Fructus Ventris Tui Jesus . . . and Benedicta Tu Es . . . In mulieribus Fructus Ventris Tuis. An endless chain of slurred words marching towards the final awakening, the motorial resurrection of a flesh still so young:

Lazarus, come forth!

"Angela, now give me your hands. Hold my hands! Hold them tighter! Just like that. Now, arise and walk. You *can* walk! Stand up, stand!"

Eyes. Those of the old woman flash, with faith or folly. Those of my friend glistening, due to something I prefer not to think about. Those of whom who keep on staring, of whom who do not know where to look, how to endure: everything, but not that red-faced little girl humiliated by her umpteenth failure. I stare back at my dolly shoes, feeling relieved and guilty at the same time. As if being able to walk or not were gifts, or punishments: some get them, others don't. Absolutely free of charge and without any merit on the part of the recipient, such as the faith which our reverend always spoke about.

"Tell me, Angela: do you believe in Jesus, do you believe in Our Lady? You'll walk, then. Now have some rest, that's enough for today; meanwhile, you keep this, and put it on your legs every night. It's holy water, from Lourdes. Next time, you'll walk."

How come no one stops this old woman? Why don't *we* stop her?

* * *

The fathers would always escape from this. They preferred to remain outside, in the cold, smoking and watching the white Fara mountains, which seemed covered with flour, the same kind we'd use to sprinkle on our manger scene during Christmas, mimicking snow. Yes, maybe some of them believed in miracles, or at least hoped in one, otherwise they wouldn't have driven us up there, but they dared not say it, that faith was a woman's thing. Angela's father, must have been an atheist, because he insisted on staying at home. Just as well: he wouldn't have to see us going out, confused, with our heads down; he would not have to hear his friends swearing, immediately muffled by the ringing protest of their wives.

"That's enough, this is the last time ever!" blurted out the most reckless and pissed off one, thinking of all those miles of petrol going up in smoke. "I already told you, that old bag is only an impostor, a fake magician . . . if anything, she might be able to remove a curse, but only Jesus Christ can work real miracles, haven't you heard what the Reverend said?"

Then his eyes fell on Angela, and he instantly became silent. Who was he to take away the hope of walking from that little, chubby blond girl? What if that was his own daughter in her place?

We suffocated our disappointment by munching down our

sandwiches, breathing the fresh, nippy mountain air deeply, taking a few paces around to stretch our legs, we who were able to do that! I was very careful not to step into the mud: I did not want to hear my mother's sermons again ("What are you wearing? It takes boots to go up there, *those* shoes are not suitable for the mountains!"). We'd set back down to the Adriatic shores, with grimaced faces, finally free, in the protective shells of our cars, to speak ill of the old woman. All were in agreement: that's it, really enough; the very last time. Yet, come next week, hope would grow back, like an inexorable cancer, and we would again make arrangements, we would again take the road back up to Fara.

* * *

Sometimes I think I know why Angela can't walk and won't walk the next time around. The Reverend has nothing to do with it, not even the old woman: they are all in good faith, each in their own little way. Sometimes, during the Rosary, I'd wander off, my lips chewing an indigestible layer of boredom; I'd rather already be at home, I'm tired of mum, of mums, of that old grumpy bag and all their recitations and I'm positive Angela would rather be in her own room as well, quiet, free from those sacred echoes in her ears, finally at peace with her immobility. I look down, comparing the sparkle of the chrome wheels of her wheelchair to the sparkle of my dolly shoes; I try to move them without others noticing, playing with the reflections of the candles.

The old woman's fat cat is snoring on the floor. That prayerful chant of ours, instead of helping him to sleep, wakes him up; annoyed, he stares at us, similar in everything to his mistress, then points straight at me. Every time I'm afraid he'll jump on me; instead, he rubs his fur on my dolly shoes, as if hypnotized by their luster. I rotate my ankles inward and, using the tip of my shoes, start to scratch him under his neck. My mom shoots me with angry stares between Hail Marys, while the purring of the cat gets stronger, but I won't chase him away: who knows, maybe Angela is looking sideways at him as well, struggling to stay serious, struggling with the Evil One who's tickling her throat.

* * *

"I'll never forget that time, we were ten: it was winter and I was locked up at home, as usual. It had been snowing for hours; I'd been watching you play outside, making snowmen, throwing snowballs at each other. How I envied you! Then you disappeared, out of the blue: your mother had obviously called you back home. But after a while, our doorbell rang, and there you were, in front of me, with a pan in your hands. That was the first time in my life I touched snow."

Angela's voice is lost in a hosanna of applause, tears, toasts, hugs. I take the microphone from her hands to replicate but I'm overcome by emotion. We fall back on a classic Italian birthday karaoke: "Io Vagabondo" becomes more out of tune with each stanza.

"What about the weekends going to the old woman in the Fara: do you remember them?" I'd like to ask her, my beautiful friend who has pulled up her blonde hair, just a shade darker than thirty years ago, and wears a mermaid dress, with a matching pair of sparkling dolly shoes leaning against the foot of her electric wheelchair. At forty, you bet as to whether she rose up and walked: college diploma, work, love, marriage, travel, adoption, friends galore. The Reverend is dead, the old woman as well. We dance like crazy, thinking about nothing, or maybe even thinking about all of this, of the miraculous movement of life, with confetti and streamers covering us lightly like flour on a manger scene in the fever of this Saturday evening. ■

Translated by Michael Kirylo

Cristina Alziati (Milan, 1963) is a poet and a translator of German literature and philosophy. Her first collection of poetry, *A compimento*, appeared in 2005 (Manni) and was awarded with the Premio Pasolini. It was followed by *Come non piangenti* in 2011 (Marcos y Marcos). Alziati's work is characteristic for its political and moral value; the author draws inspiration from the news, politics, and her private life to investigate a reality that is permeated by incredible suffering and mysterious beauty. These topics become the starting point for observations and meditations whose scope unfurls from the here and now in universal, timeless ripples. All this presents a unique mixture of stylistic opposites that harmoniously come together to create surprising, lively results: a solemn tone, classical and biblical references united with a verse that is dry, austere and yet musical. Among her influences in Italian literature, critics have mentioned Vittorio Sereni, Eugenio Montale, and most importantly Franco Fortini.

The following poems are from the collection *Come non piangenti.*

TO MY FATHER
Cristina Alziati

You took a bath, put on fresh clothes,
then at every step my mind slides away.
I didn't want to see you,
I'm sure they laid you out.
I just want to know, unless it was a dream,
that your meticulous attention was not
anguish—the documents you laid on the bench,
the chair you carried into the garden, the knot—
but some unknowable, yet bearable,
condition. It all rests with you, undisclosed.
Perhaps to leaven its weight, I preserve,
of your act, its other aspect—the thud
of the chair on stone, and your absence,
and the sway, which I rock, slowly and more slowly,
of the body beneath the pergola.

Translated by Robert Hahn and Michela Martini

THE CHEMO CURLS

Cristina Alziati

"Give me back my love," she will croon,
fastened to the chemo bags,
and Orpheus too; but cycle
after cycle that song unravels,
and the sun and the underworld. To see the stars again
—she will tell him—he needs to get himself out.
She stays where she is, Euridice. Everything
truly does happen, forever.

1

How do you want me to speak of the months
of that strange, extraordinary winter,
of buds even up here, and sun
among the branches in December, when I was
the layer of snow, the naked bark,
the squeak of frost in the bones—with what
extraordinary voice tell you of the winter,
when I was the winter?

2

"Momma, you've turned into the puppy,"
Sophia cried, after the haircut, before
the first chemotherapy cycle—nothing
to it: from her bubbling laughter
I was born again, a different person,
my daughter's daughter.

3

"Now rise again." This voice, I know,
was Beppe, I didn't grasp it, I was
a hat on a head, a
figure that for a certain truce,
a different ending imagined, the railing,
the sudden wreck—like that,
it was a matter of me saying farewell
to myself, greeting the new me,
survivor of disease—

4

Voices on the phone I heard faintly,
I always pulled it down over my ears
—even at night, to keep
my head warm, it was cold
outside the head, inside it was hot, my dear
friend asked me from Paris: are you writing?
What's happening now is not worth writing.
"Write"—Beppe said—
"rise now. Write." I didn't get it.

5

Surely I was still among the ferns,
the sky, and the hide-and-seek, flying
with the flocks; until that voice
I was eternal—the voice
inside the hospital, in the room,
in a foreign language
affirmed strange data, an unending
truth: where there used to be one,
there within me, there wasn't one;
the scalpel defined precisely
the dying self revealed within me.

6

Rise now. Close your book. Go out.
Go through the passages of rain, among the drops.
What has the will to survive will live.
You still want to know where the nipple
has gone, what happens to the flesh, what company
gets rid of it, where it all goes, how it gets
disposed of, this hazardous waste,
you still want to speak to the surgeon,
the maestro of sutures, who has taken strips
of your skin and stitched up
your soul's debris.

to G.

7

"We won't meet any more"—within a voice
as pale as porcelain I poured out my tears,
within the cracks of a mute terror.

You heard me out as we sat beside
that wide window, watching the sky.
I heard your offhand *who knows* as a promise.

8

And then, on this side, slowly,
confused by the skin in tatters,
echoes returned, unless it was a dream,
of other bombardments.
You're not confused, it is history
that breaks us apart. And inside that, inside
every hour of the world you hear
time moaning for the time that remains.

Translated by Robert Hahn and Michela Martini

REBUS

Rosebud Rosabella

Nicola Skert, born in a remote Italian village on the border of Austria, has a scientific background and as a biologist has published several scientific articles. He has also published short stories in various anthologies, the noir novel *Pus Underground* (Montag) in 2010, the collection of tales *PET (Pulp Erotic Trash) vol. 1* (Lettere Animate)—created, as the author says, "with the express purpose of putting a strain on public morals"—in 2013, and not to mention the novel *Hitorizumo* (Minerva, 2013), currently in the top twenty best-selling science fiction books in Italy and gaining a lot of attention from both critics and readers. Given the highly cinematic aspect of this novel, while waiting for someone to decide to produce the film, several teasers were made and shown on YouTube. Skert is currently living in a city in northern Italy, where he continues his literary production.

The following is an excerpt from *Hitorizumo*.

HITORIZUMO

Nicola Skert

They reached a crossroad that gave onto a wider straighter road. Around them, a heavy silence wrapped in frozen nothingness. No source of light. No trace of humanity. Only a frozen animal, close to the crossroads, in its hunched corpse a looming message of death. It was so completely curled up on itself, as though in final defense against the cold it had slowly sucked itself dry, it was no longer possible to tell what it was: a large dog, a young wild boar, an unimportant distraction to relieve the mind. Mirko slowed and detaching his eyes from the frozen carcass, checked the map.

"We've taken a hell of a deviation!" he commented. "Here it says we must do another fifty kilometres."

"We'll do it," Paul reassured him, "d'you want me to drive?"

"No way, I've had enough of your off-roading."

"We'll probably have to do even more," Paul replied. "D'you feel like facing the drive?" There followed a short silence, after which, shaking his head, Mirko gave up the wheel.

"Okay, you drive," he said, sounding contrary.

Mirko released his seatbelt, exaggerating the movement as though in protest. They set off in silence. Paul threw a glance at the two indicators, those he was the most interested in, and both gave out bad news. The tank was already three quarters empty, and at minus fifteen the climate was becoming a threat, grasping the environment in its icy grip, the air becoming even drier, the atmosphere crystallising, covering bushes, fields and meadows with a whitish patina. No one was to be seen, whoever might still be left alive was too busy trying to keep warm somewhere; taking refuge in dark cold shelters that had once been homes. The only present danger was from the icy roads and Paul asked himself if there might be snow chains in the car. He shivered at the very thought of having to put them on in that cold; he'd never done it before. Anyway, if it was necessary he would ask Mirko. At least he would be useful for something he told himself, with an unfair spurt of anger.

They continued for some time immersed in their own worries and hopes, until Mirko pointed something out ahead of them. Their faces betrayed a cautious hope. On the horizon, on the other side of a long line of hills, the sky was lit up by an elongated reddish glow, flat and disc-shaped.

"It looks like . . . it looks like the dawn!" Mirko suggested. "The dawn through the clouds, on the horizon! Maybe we're coming out, the sun's rising!"

"I don't want to seem rude, but look over there," said Paul, showing the compass that he'd pulled out of his rucksack pocket. "D'you really think a north-west sunrise is possible?"

"Well, why not?" Mirko threw back, "After all everything's been turned on its head."

"Look, let's try not to lose our minds! It's only three in the afternoon . . . Jesus! Three in the afternoon. I told Angela I'd be back by eleven at the latest . . . I'm four hours late!"

"You'll see, we'll get there soon . . ." Mirko tried to reassure him. ". . . Shouldn't be much further now."

"I hope not. Just the thought that they're at home alone, makes me crazy."

"I know. That's why we must keep our heads, okay? Anyway, that glow of light is on our way home, who knows maybe things are better there, perhaps they've got electric generators . . ."

Paul didn't argue and in the silence Mirko shared the same thought. In reality both of them guessed what that streak of light vibrating on the crest of the hills could be, even if unconsciously trying to ignore it. On reaching the foot of the hills, where they began to penetrate the seemingly urban territory, the more hostile and inhospitable the streets appeared. Climbing the hill steeply, they were forced to slow down, zig zagging between abandoned cars, some of which had crashed, others reduced to burnt out wrecks. There wasn't a soul alive and in a way an explanation wasn't necessary, from that moment it was easy to guess that things were only going to get worse. More than once they were forced to stop, faced with the icy cold and risk of ambush, pushing cars that blocked their way off the road. The main thing was to go on, at any cost, and anyway no one was about to protest: they were too busy just trying to survive. They looked at the houses that lined the street with their hearts in their mouths. They all gave off the same air of total abandonment. Dark, barred, empty of any life that would give warmth, life, continuity.

At times the main road was so blocked with deserted cars and various pieces of debris that they were forced to take long deviations by side roads. Yet more gasoline thrown away with wasted energy and heat. Of course it would have crossed their minds to syphon some off from the disorderly abandoned vehicles along the road, if someone else hadn't already had the same idea. There wasn't a petrol cap in sight that wasn't opened. To their eyes they were like "no go" road signs put out along the road always giving the same information: stop—tank empty—try the next vehicle.

When they got to the top of the hill, as though in reward for the difficulties they had overcome, they were met with an incredibly powerful spectacle. Paul stopped the car, his face reflecting a reddish blaze lighting up the car interior from the left. In front of them, split in two by the formation of the hills, the remainder of the boundless plains opened up. Over the centuries, in the center of the distended lowlands, a city had been built, prospering, growing, supplied by industry and intensive agriculture. It had a well-preserved historical center, surrounded by ancient walls, a well-liked and densely populated area, and spacious green areas. A continuously evolving urban jewel.

Now, it was wrapped in an immense ball of fire.

Advancing from the north it was heading slowly towards them in a long line of extremely high flames. Without other means of keeping going, over dozens of kilometres it was attacking not only urban districts but also nearby fields and woodlands right up to the industrial zone from where enormous columns of fire illuminated the sky; mushroom-shaped explosions followed by a blast causing the glass in the car windows to vibrate. The huge expanse was a single hellish ocean that boiled and heaved its inflamed waves towards them in search of other material to burn. The clouds that had withheld the light, reflecting it onto the ground, forming the dawn-like effect that had briefly eluded them, were in reality powerful billows of smoke. Only the river that cut through the plains and crossed the burning city ran on slowly and forcefully in its meandering; seemingly indifferent to the tragedy touching its banks. Hell reflected in its surface, floating up and down, a flaming boat along its shores. The people were searching for light, light and warmth, and were doing everything possible to get it, whatever the consequences.

"Look down there," Mirko prompted, pointing an index finger

towards the hillside.

Below them, the fire was about to assault the remaining city outskirts. Crowds of individuals surged on the edges of the fire. Paul drew out a powerful binocular from his rucksack and aimed it forwards in search of the underlying zone. Though silenced by the distance, he could clearly make out the ant-like crowd below, and his jaw dropped in horror. It wasn't a human mass on the run. The individuals of which it was made up were there, just a dozen meters from the fire, trying to make the most of the heat and light it gave out. Behind, total darkness, which no one dared to enter.

Some kindled neighboring houses with lit torches, probably without even asking themselves if anyone was still in them. He saw a human torch throwing itself out of a building, another from a window in a high apartment block. Slowly Paul lowered the binoculars.

". . . you wanna look?" he demanded in a broken voice.

"No, thanks. Your face is enough. And I don't like what's written on it."

"So that's why we met no one on the road. Like us, they headed in the direction of the light source, feeding it with what they could."

"They're dyin' like flies down there, aren't they?" Mirko demanded.

"Like flies drawn to a deadly light," reflected Paul, then in a loud voice: "We must get going and climb over that wall of fire."

"Oh that's great! And how d' you think we're gonna do that? Go around it? It's dozens of kilometers of road that we don't even know, probably barricaded, with thousands of traps . . ."

"We'll get to the fire, find a boat that's working, go up the river and get behind the line of fire."

"You're mad. Of all the crazy ideas . . ."

A sharp blow behind them interrupted the debate. A heavy, blunt instrument had struck the back window, splintering it. A second blow was trying to enlarge the crack that was appearing. Meanwhile, someone was forcing the closed side door, yet another violent blow found the car roof, bending it inwards. A full force assault, well coordinated, from many sides. ■

Translated by Deborah Davies

Fabio Donalisio was born in 1977 near Turin. He now lives in Rome, and is a poet, translator, and journalist (and occasionally a Latin teacher in public high schools). His book reviews appear in music magazines such as *Blowup* and *Rolling Stone Italia*. He also published his poetry in *miti logiche* (Excogita, 2007), and *la pratica del ritorno* (*Poesia contemporanea, XI quaderno italiano*, Marcos y Marcos, 2012). He wrote a post scriptum to the Italian edition of *Bad Seed* by Ian Johnston, Odoya, 2012.

The following poems are from *La pratica del ritorno* and were (re)written in English by the author.

(to himself)

Fabio Donalisio

and mud is the world
maybe a mode, a mourn
a chance of road
even vague, vain

(*…or not to be*)

being glad of deserts
this remains beyond collapses
mistakes and the time so tall

and (obvious, yes)
the endless vanity of it all

Translated by the author

(manifestino)

Fabio Donalisio

I claim the right to being fickle
to the broken line, the hole
the tickle
contumacy as form and substance
of a word-thing that still knows
some rage and most of all
not bed, nor late
I claim beyond a me, or a you
I vote life against work, too

(‘cause a poet is, you *see*, a spoken
fate, as cruel as it can be

Translated by the author

[unbelievably alone]

Fabio Donalisio

you can believe in the dark when the light lies

unbelievably alone
that is I don't believe it
even and mostly
as I see with the eyes

and the simple reasons for the ticket
go down with the flight

Translated by the author

[some things are gaping]

Fabio Donalisio

there is a crack in everything, that's how the light gets in
l.c.

some things are gaping
or half closed, drafts perhaps, even murmurs
being paid in full is an accounting concept
or—even if you count—a showdown
the seal is god's stuff (he who
forbids, who doesn't say but said)
and the light, everywhere,
enters kind of a blade

Translated by the author

(ROME)

Fabio Donalisio

look,
the eternal jest city takes up
the thread of round, very
reasonable speeches
repays feeble tolls
to the wonder of worlds
that she, insane, founds

and,
if she even shoots
—hopes,
just play it dumb (you can)
it's just a pat on the ass
—marble hard —
of the West

Translated by the author

NEVER AGAIN

Mauro Castellani

Nicola Manuppelli is a novelist, poet, and essayist, as well as a translator and editor of American literature in Italy. His translations include the works of Andre Dubus, Chuck Rosenthal, Charles Baxter, Larry Brown, A. B. Guthrie, Robert Ward, Lee Maynard, Willa Cather, Ernest Gaines, Edward Field, William J. Harris, and many others. He wrote an unofficial biography of Alice Munro, *La fessura* (Barbera, 2014). His first novel, *Bowling*, was released in 2014 by Barney. His short stories have appeared in many anthologies. He is currently completing the official biography of the American writer Chuck Kinder and writing *The losers*, a series of five novels, including *A hotel called imagination*, from which this excerpt is taken. He lives in Milan.

SUMMER!

Nicola Manuppelli

The open front door sent a blade of light into the building lobby. Just outside, a good number of folks stood unmoving. V. himself, getting out, gave a slow turn, the soles of his shoes grinding against the tile of the stoop's top step. He glimpsed others gathered on the opposite side of the street, not much of a group. The ones having fun, it looked like, were the children, while their mothers appeared more concerned with protecting their eyes from the sun and dabbing the sweat off their faces. He didn't see more than a few men.

The noise kept on, deafening. Nearly all the kids were waving candy canes, their coils of hard sugar either red or sky blue. These were given out by girls in uniform, a blue top and white skirt, who must've preceded the band. The players themselves must've called a halt, perhaps on the next street over, in order to show off what they could do.

One of the uniformed girls came his way, holding out a candy-cane. She said nothing, limiting herself to a bright smile and an offer of a new color, peach at the top. V. shook his head. The girl shifted away.

The sugar smell mixed with that of fried goods, coming down from the occasional open window above the little square—Ocean, surely—and rendered the very air artificial. Then outside this square, this Ocean, they'd set up stalls, the food quick and handy, with plenty of nuts and pastry, the usual sweets.

He searched his pockets and came up with a cigarette, slowing down, waiting. All this commotion had to mean that something more was about to take place, and you had to think this meant the band. Yet the faces around him were concentrating so intently that these people seemed to be expecting a lot more than a marching band: an escape route, permission to go.

The players arrived from his left. They must've started on

a perpendicular leading down into this Ocean, up where V. had glimpsed, in the light, some flags and bunting strung between posts. The decorations revealed cornucopia designs and a word or two about *summer*. WELCOME, SUMMER! Now the entire band was around the corner, coming at V.. At first they'd suggested no more than a frail rain of dust at the end of the street, but then the bodies took shape; the music started up once more. Louder still, enormous. Within the hilltop piazza, the notes echoed, confused, sounding less like any melody and more like an unhinged noise, in which every instrument went off in its own direction. Around V., everyone had their eyes fixed on the point where the uproar seemed to start. Eventually he, too, saw.

The musicians had on suits of a dense, blinding red, except the collars, a golden yellow that suggested war medals, and the boots, shining and black. They marched slowly, mechanically, with that rain of dust suspended in the air before them. They must've been hot, dolled up like that, and their faces looked skeletal, gray and drawn. Altogether they suggested something sordid, though V. couldn't think what that might be. Certainly their playing remained tuneless, out of synch, and every now and then one of them threw a nasty glance. A number appeared awfully old for this, and a number were still children. This one playing the cymbals, for instance—he couldn't have been more than a child.

Or perhaps this boy was as much as fourteen. Perhaps it was just that his close-cut hair made him look younger than he was. He had a disrespectful face, taunting, that seemed more suited to a comic book. He enjoyed turning that wicked smile on the ladies lining the streets, the girls as well as the women, and they reacted as if they were in on the joke. The boy's build was wispy, but he had muscled-up arms. He didn't just play the cymbals, he bashed away as if they were at war with each other, with no more rhythm than if he were slapping together the soles of two oversized shoes, practically enraged, sending up a tremendous racket. He could've been one of those windup dolls that move only arms, legs, and head, with his two eyes bulging. His jacket didn't fit, it was too small, and his arms were naked almost halfway up, revealing wrists and more, all covered with an orange down.

The other players kept their distance from this boy, they created a hole in their ranks, no doubt to avoid getting mowed down by those cymbals, those arms. In fact as the band had moved on, this one had kept falling further behind, finally winding up at the rear of the group. By now he'd begun playing with the onlookers along the street. He'd pause, holding his cymbals suspended above him, then all of a sudden crash them together, completely ignoring the beat or the tune. All with an infernal smile.

V. noticed a girl about the same age with short blonde hair and a white skirted outfit, soft as a sheet. An outfit such as a tennis player might wear. The girl grew red, blushing, as this boy in red swung by. He gave her a nod and somehow, with one hand, gave a gesture that could only mean they'd see each other later.

The girl stepped back, holding down her skirt with both hands.

Now the Charleston rhythm asserted itself, louder still, actually syncopated. Even the girls selling candy canes had started to dance, along the edges of the band, their ill-cut gowns swinging, their small necklaces popping out from under their tops. Some were pearl, glittering, almost billiard balls in bright sun.

Suddenly everything seemed sequined, dazzling, bejeweled. It was the sky, a blue so intense it made the other colors pop, like a photographer's special effect.

Then there was the man at the head of the parade, huffing and puffing into a big tuba. His swollen cheeks were as red as his jacket, though in his case the jacket wore a word in white stitching: *Ocean*. Also the jacket's shoulders had flowers attached, in a range of colors. The guy's hands were covered in sweat, and his hair, white, was plastered to his forehead. It looked like he might topple over any minute. His wrinkles might've been a spiderweb that covered him from face to arms to lower legs: those calves you saw poking out of pants cut short, improbably short. He was the only one wearing a unit that didn't quite match the others, seeming in some way an outsider in the band, an add-on. Yet he was at the front, as if dragged into it by the others up there, the man on the big bass drum and two young players, one on trumpet and the other on clarinet. Each had the same receding hairline, their heads gleaming of course, and their legs followed a tight rhythm, pumping up and down; even their rumps moved as one.

The whole arrangement seemed without focus or guidelines, a hodge-podge.

Mr. Big Tuba, at least, looked genuinely focused on what he was doing. His horn appeared gilded, though touched with rust at the lip, and it wound around him like a seashell—or perhaps a serpent.

Ahead of them all, up beyond even the tuba, was the biggest person on the piazza, an enormous man. He wore a black frock-tail coat, flashy with rhinestones, sparkling in the sun, and a peaked hat, also black, as he waved a baton. His movement was casual, as if he were only pretending to direct this "orchestra." Mostly he had his back to the players, too—but when he turned to face them, the music grew louder. He had his face done up like a clown, with a fake red nose and plenty of white pancake. He'd taken care of his eyes with black liner.

The man couldn't be the actual conductor. All the makeup turned the expression grotesque, but he continued to smile. A few of the youngest, the babies in the crowd, started to cry as he approached. Meanwhile the clown pulled what looked like big blue flower petals from his jacket pocket and tossed these to a couple of the ladies.

By now the four-four of the Charleston had become a mad dance, always more jagged. The faces of those on trumpet and clarinet had gone purple, and all over the piazza the mingled odors of sweet goods and fried had grown sharper, sickly. Overhead a cloud might've passed, but in its wake the sun and heat grew worse. Someone was singing, somewhere, the words indistinguishable.

V. found he hadn't moved from outside his entryway. The phony conductor had pulled up before him, and he could see that in one of the big man's jacket pockets, the one from which he'd pulled the flower petals, there now poked up the neck of a bottle.

The immense clown was wheeling left and right, saying hi to the children, when his eyes found V.'s. With that he reached into his jacket, almost causing the bottle to drop from its pocket, and pulled out some sort of poster or placard. This was crumpled, naturally, and the conductor's hands shook as he unfolded it. The paper proved enormous, almost too much even for so large a jacket.

It could've been a magic trick, and around V. people gasped: *ohhh* . . . The youngest got excited, especially those with candy cane smears all over their faces. A few weren't paying attention, taking advantage of the ruckus to fool around with a Hula-Hoop at a nearby street corner. They moved slowly, though, under the brutal sun. They'd found a cooler spot, by the trash cans, and all these kids wore some kind of cap, protection against sunstroke.

"Summer sales!" cried the clown. "Big, big discounts!" He held up the unfolded placard: a wide yellow rectangle with paste-ons of local goods.

Applause and howls, and then one rising, strident voice, a man's voice that for a moment drowned out the music.

"Open up!" he screamed.

"Yes, yes," shouted another. "Open up!"

"No question!" This voice came from across the street. "Do it!"

The street before V. had pretty much broken into pandemonium, the onlookers rushing in among the squawking band. You'd think the clown couldn't be heard, but he broke into a scream:

"Summertime!" he bellowed. "Summertime!"

"So, do it!" erupted another voice. "Open the place!"

"Right away!"

Harsh whistles, derisive, mixed with new applause. People were waving their arms, holding up money, banknotes big and small. Meantime the odors of sweets and oils bore down, clogging the nostrils, always more bitter and harder to take.

V. tossed his cigarette to the ground. He'd had enough.

As he crushed the butt beneath his heel, the band regrouped and lurched forward once more, all twenty or so players together. They stopped before the big shopping center at one end of the piazza, meantime wrapping up the Charleston. Instead they went into a kind of march: PA-RA PAM, PA-PA, PA-RA PAM!

Up went the rattling gates of the mall. Out came another vast *Ohhhh . . .*

V. couldn't help giving the scene another look. Inside the shops' entrance a neon sign came on, announcing that they had air conditioning. Out in the piazza the women and children were wheeling round as if in river eddies, flowing towards the mall. The howls continued, amid clusters of shoving and squabbling.

"It's summer," a woman shouted. "It's the arrival of summer!"

The words made him notice her red mouth, roughly smeared with shreds of lipstick like bits of leftover bubblegum. Yet the lips themselves, beneath all that gloss, maintained their softness, their flesh. V. believed he'd known lips like that.

Amid the din the woman turned to him, her eyes burning orange.

"Cover your ears," the woman said.

"What?"

"I told you, cover your *ears*!" ■

Translated by John Domini

NOTES ON TRANSLATORS AND ARTISTS

Traci Andrighetti, PhD, is a linguist with a passion for Italian language and culture. After serving as lecturer of Italian at the University of Texas at Austin for eleven years, she left academia to work for Apple Inc., where she is a content writer and editor. She is also a prize-winning literary translator, a published author of articles about translation, foreign language education and linguistics, and an editor of academic, business, and literary manuscripts. In 2011, she created *italicissima*, an award-winning bilingual blog about Italy's dialects and the varieties and forms of Italian employed in contemporary literature. In 2014 she published *Limoncello Yellow*, the first novel in the Franki Amato Mysteries.

Jacob Blakesley is a Leverhulme Early Career Fellow at the University of Leeds's Center for Translation Studies. His recent monograph is entitled *Modern Italian Poets: Translators of the Impossible*, published by the University of Toronto Press (2014). He has also translated an anthology of modern Italian fiction for Dover Publications, *Great Italian Short Stories of the Twentieth Century* (2013).

Margaret Brose is Professor Emerita of Italian and Comparative Literature at the University of California, Santa Cruz. She earned her PhD in Romance languages at Harvard University and has previously taught at the University of Colorado at Boulder and at Yale University. She has received numerous teaching awards and fellowships, among which are a Fulbright, NEH, ACLS, and a residency at the American Academy of Rome. Professor Brose has written widely on all periods of Italian literature. Her book *Leopardi sublime: la poetica della temporalità* won the MLA Marraro-Scaglione prize for the best book in Italian literary studies in 2000. She has published translations of several contemporary Italian poets (Patrizia Cavalli, Biancamaria Frabotta, Eugenio Montale) and was one of the contributors to the first complete English translation of Leopardi's notebooks, *Lo Zibaldone* (Farrar Straus Giroux, 2013). She is presently working on the translation of Leopardi's youthful writings, *Frammenti autobiografici.*

Mauro Castellani was born in 1953 in Serre di Rapolano (Siena), and now lives in Florence. He has a Master's in Chemistry and Pharmaceutical Technologies, and he worked in the molecular medicine field for a while. He has experience in different branches of visual arts: painting, advertisement, jewelry design. He has completed several photo shootings in Europe, America, Asia, and the Middle East. At the moment he is deepening his knowledge of painting at the Accademia di Belle Arti of Florence.

Bonnie Costello is a professor of English at Boston University. She has written many books and articles on modern poetry; her most recent book is *Planets on Tables: Poetry, Still Life and the Turning World* (Cornell, 2008). She also publishes essays on art, travel, and memoir. Her translations of Italian poetry have appeared in *Literary Imagination, Journal of Italian Translation*, and *Faultline*. She would like to thank Adriana Keseru for her help in checking translations for accuracy.

Deborah Davies, born in England, has been living and working in a beautiful part of Northern Italy for the last nine years. As an English specialist and cofounder of the English-speaking cultural club OutandAbout, she organizes events, workshops, and presentations in English in many fields, including theater and cinema, literature, history and art, and food and drink. She also works with professionals and companies on improving communication skills, preparing for international presentations, and translating scripts and texts into English. She does not consider herself a translator in the traditional sense, preferring to work closely with the writer to capture and express the very meaning of their words in the English language. At present she is writing a book on the history and intangible cultural heritage of the region where she lives.

John Domini's latest book, *The Sea-God's Herb*, a selection of criticism, appeared in 2014 from Dzanc Books. His translation of *Books & Rough Business* by Tullio Pironti appeared in 2009 from Red Hen Press. Over the next two years, Dzanc will publish a sequence of short stories, *MOVIEOLA!*, and the novel *The Color Inside a Melon*. A collection of Domini's poetry, *The Grand McLuckless Road Atlas*, was published in 2013. Other work has appeared in *The Paris Review*, *Ploughshares*, *GQ*, the *New York Times*, and many anthologies. Both print and electronic versions of his earlier novels and story collections are available. He has received fellowships from the National Endowment for the Arts and elsewhere.

Rudi Dundas is a photographer focused on social change and environmental issues. She photographed wild tulips in the Tien Shan Mountains for Michael Pollan's film, "Botany of Desire," as well as in Rwanda, Ethiopia, Uganda, Tanzania, Malawi, and Indonesia covering sustainable farming for Peet's Coffee, US AID, and others. She has photographed extensively in Ethiopia, Uganda, Kenya and West Bengal for drinking water issues. Rudi worked at the Gobelins in Paris, and in NYC creating tapestries based upon her photographic images. From 1989-1995, she was co-director of a non-profit gallery in Soho in New York City. A recipient of fellowships from the NEA, New York Foundation for the Arts and the Adobe Foundation, she was nominated for a Lucie Award for international photography in 2014. Rudi served on the board of directors of *Artforum* magazine for twenty years and currently serves on the board of The American Photographic Artists in San Francisco.

Adam Elgar's poems and verse translations have appeared in a range of journals including *Poetry Review*, *Stand*, the *Keats-Shelley Review*, *Warwick Review*, *Magma*, *Orbis*, and *Iota*. His poetry collection *Temporali* was published in 2007 by Lopside Press. His translation of Alessandra Lavagnino's novella *Truth and Flies* is published by Troubador Storia, and his translations of her stories have appeared in *Stand* and *New Walk Review*. The opening chapters of Lavagnino's *The Mother of the Last Prophet*, a novella about John the Baptist and his parents, were published in *Comparative Critical Studies* in 2014. Elgar's ongoing translation of the complete Don Camillo stories by Giovanni Guareschi is being published by Pilot Productions. He translates for *The International Journal of Psychoanalysis* and for the Vatican Museums, and until 2013 he was the translation moderator at the online literary forum, Eratosphere.

Adria Frizzi teaches Italian at the University of Texas at Austin. She writes about and translates contemporary fiction from Italy and Latin America. She has translated Osman Lins's *Nine, Novena* (Sun and Moon Press, 1995; Green Integer, 2010) and *The Queen of the Prisons of Greece* (Dalkey Archive Press, 1995), Caio Fernando Abreu's *Whatever Happened to Dulce Veiga?* (University of Texas Press, 2000), and *Regina Rheda's Stories from the Copan Building* (*First World, Third Class*, University of Texas Press, 2005). Other authors she has translated include Dacia Maraini, Elena Ferrante, and Marina Colasanti. She has completed, with co-translator Traci Andrighetti, the translation manuscript of Rossana Campo's *Mai sentita cosi' bene* (*Never Felt So Good*).

Georgia Emma Gili received her MA in Literature and Philosophy from Anglia Ruskin University, Cambidge, UK. She has been working in Italy as an English language teacher and translator since 1998.

Robert Hahn is a poet and essayist as well as a translator. His books of poetry include *No Messages* (University of Notre Dame) and *All Clear* (University of South Carolina). His essays have appeared in the *American Scholar*, *Kenyon Review*, *TriQuarterly*, *Yale Review*, *Parnassus*, *Southern Review*, *Film Quarterly*, *Southwest Review*, *Sewanee Review*, *Michigan Quarterly Review*, *Southern Humanities Review*, *Antioch Review*, and other journals. His writing on translation includes essays on Charles Wright in Italian (Parnassus) and Louise Gluck in Italian. He is currently completing a companion essay on Charles Simic in Italian. His honors include an NEA Fellowship, the *Southwest Review* Best Essay Award, a Notable Essay in Best *American Essays*, the Sandeen Award (University of Notre Dame), the Keats-Shelley Poetry Prize (England), and residency fellowships at MacDowell and Bogliasco (Italy). He lives in Boston.

As an American citizen born and raised in Tuscany by American-Dutch parents, **Michael Kirylo** has always been interested in exploring the clash between different cultures and ways of life. He spent years traveling and living in the Far East and Europe before getting back to Italy and settling down in the Abruzzi region. Passionate about scuba diving and swimming as well as about religion, philosophy, and world history, he's been working as a multilingual customer services officer and commercial translator. Only recently has he applied his language skills to literary translation: the Anglo-American version of Franca Di Muzio's "Arise and Walk" is his first work of that kind.

Michela Martini, a native of Genoa, Italy, received her MA in Italian literature from the University of Genoa, where she studied with Edoardo Sanguineti. She has taught Italian language and culture at Suffolk University, Indiana University, Cabrillo College, and the University of California at Santa Cruz. Her translations of Italian poetry, also in collaboration with poet Robert Hahn, have appeared in the *Chicago Quarterly Review*, *Catamaran Literary Reader*, the *Literary Review, Poetry International*, *Gradiva*, *Journal of Italian Translation*, *Italian*

Poetry Review, *Literary Imagination*, *International Poetry Review*, *Unsplendid*, *etc*., and were anthologized by Geoff Brock in *The FSG Book of 20th-Century Italian Poetry*, published by Farrar, Straus and Giroux in 2014. She is currently working as a translator and editor specializing in information technology, literature, and photography.

Having grown up in a multilingual home where Italian, Spanish, English and German were spoken, **Silvana Mastrolia** developed a passion for languages from an early age. This fueled her desire to study linguistics, and she ultimately received a BA from Rutgers University, where she majored in Italian with a minor in European history. She has also participated in cognitive linguistic research as applicable to the development of speech therapy for bilingual aphasics at the Aidekman Center for Molecular and Behavioral Neuroscience in Newark, New Jersey. After employment with Immigration as a congressional liaison and interpreter, and experience as a corporate translator of journalism, and medical and engineering literature, she parlayed her knowledge into a career as a freelance translator. Subsequently, she has held the position of external quality manager at Transperfect International, where she taught herself to read Slavic and Germanic languages for the purposes of editing translations; in addition, she is a translator of French, German, Italian, Portuguese, and Spanish, and an interpreter of Italian, French, and Spanish. Currently, she is teaching English as a second language at the Nile Language School in East Rutherford, New Jersey. She is also the text editor of *TECHNĒ*, the official annual architectural journal for New York City College of Technology (CUNY).

Elizabeth McKenzie has a novel forthcoming from Penguin Press in 2016, *The Portable Veblen*. Her fiction has appeared in *The New Yorker*, *The Atlantic Monthly*, *Best American Nonrequired Reading*, and others; her stories have been performed at Symphony Space in New York and Stories on Stage in Chicago and recorded for NPR's *Selected Shorts*. Her story collection *Stop That Girl* was short-listed for The Story Prize. Her novel *MacGregor Tells the World* was a *Chicago Tribune* best book of the year and a *San Francisco Chronicle* notable book. She is currently senior editor of the *Chicago Quarterly Review* and managing editor of *Catamaran Literary Reader*.

Ellen Nerenberg is Hollis Professor of Romance Languages & Literatures at Wesleyan University, where she has taught Italian studies since 1994. She is the author of *Prison Terms: Representing Confinement During and After Italian Fascism* (University of Toronto Press, 2001), winner of the Howard R. Marraro Prize from the Modern Language Association. She co-edited *Writing Beyond Fascism: Resistance in the Life and Work of Alba de Cespedes* (Fairleigh-Dickinson University Press, 2000) and served as the co-translator and editor of Marco Baliani's *Body of State. The Moro Affair, a Nation Divided* (Fairleigh-Dickinson University Press, 2011). Her study of three acclaimed murder cases in contemporary Italy, *Murder Made in Italy: Homicide, Media, and Contemporary Italian Culture* (Indiana University Press), was published in 2012. She serves as the reviews editor for *The Journal of Italian Cinema and Media Studies* and is associate editor of *g/s/i: gender/sexuality/Italy*. Work in progress includes a book-length study of performance in, and in relation to, the work of Primo Levi. She holds degrees from Stanford University and the University of Chicago.

Katia Pansa just obtained her PhD in Italian Studies at Stanford. In her dissertation titled *Malinconia e Umorismo: il comico intellettuale nella prosa italiana del Nocevento* she proposes the aesthetic of a particular type of the comic mode, one that stands out from other types of the comic, primarily the carnivalesque, for its alliance between humor and melancholy. This alliance is realized in a manner both playful and cerebral: an intellectual lightness amidst the heaviness of modern life. In her work, Pansa puts most emphasis on the expressions of this comic mode in the prose works of the twentieth-century writers Aldo Palazzeschi and Tommaso Landolfi. The Palazzeschi-Landolfi pair offers especially valuable material for comparison in that, while both use the light comic mode, they do so from otherwise contrasting theoretical positions: the avant-garde in the case of the former, mannerism of the latter. Currently in Taiwan, Pansa is developing an interest in a comparative history of humor, driven by the question of how different experiences of modernization—the European and the Chinese—bring forth and are shaped by different conceptions and practices of literary humor.

Alta L. Price runs a New York–based editorial consultancy specializing in literature and non-fiction texts on art, architecture, design, and culture. She translates from Italian and German into English, and was awarded the 2013 Gutekunst Prize for her translation of Dea Loher's novel *Bugatti taucht auf / Bugatti Turns Up*, which was also shortlisted for the German Book Prize. She contributes to *Progetto grafico* and several other journals, and her most recent book publications include the English-language editions of Corrado Augias's *Secrets of Italy*

(Rizzoli Ex Libris, 2014), illustrator Beppe Giacobbe's *Visionary Dictionary* (Lazy Dog Press, 2013), and Marco Biraghi's *Project of Crisis: Manfredo Tafuri and the Crisis of Modernism* (MIT Press, 2013). Her translation of *Blickfang*, Jürgen Holstein's landmark tome on book cover and dust jacket design in the Weimar Republic, is forthcoming from Taschen. She loves puzzles, translation being her favorite kind. Although her soul belongs in Rome, she also organizes a biennial study tour in northern Italy for graphic designers and bibliophiles. When not at her desk translating, she's out scouting for great new stories to bring into English.

Frederika Randall was born in Pittsburgh and lives with her family in Rome, Italy. She works as a cultural journalist for both English and Italian language publications and has translated novels by Luigi Meneghello (his classic, *Deliver Us*), Ottavio Cappellani (*Sicilian Tragedee*), Helena Janeczek (*The Swallows of Monte Cassino*), and Italy's great epic of the Risorgimento, Ippolito Nievo's *Confessions of an Italian*. Among other works in her translations are historian Sergio Luzzatto's book-length essay, *The Body of Il Duce*, and his *Padre Pio: Miracles and Politics in a Secular Age*, for which she and the author shared the Cundill Prize for History for the English version in 2011. Her translation of Luzzatto's *Partigia*, about Primo Levi's experience as a partisan, is due out in 2015, and she is now translating Guido Morselli's *Il comunista* for New York Review Books. She received a PEN (Heim) Translation Fund Award in 2009 and was a Bogliasco Fellow with the Liguria Center for the Arts and Humanities in 2013.

Rosebud Rosabella is the longing for something lost a long time ago and the impossibility of fitting it into the allotted space.

Olivia E. Sears is founder of the Center for the Art of Translation (www.catranslation.org), a non-profit organization that champions literary translation and cultural diversity through Two Lines Press books and through its education program, Poetry Inside Out, teaching children to write and translate poetry. For more than a decade, she edited the annual anthology *Two Lines: World Writing in Translation*, which she founded in 1993. As a translator of Italian poetry, she has published work by Patrizia Cavalli, Tiziano Rossi, Maria d'Arezzo, and Ardengo Soffici, as well as Renaissance women poets Veronica Gambara and Vittoria Colonna. She is a frequent collaborator with visual artist Aline Mare on multimedia poetry performances and installations about science and the natural world, most recently *photo/synthesis*. She holds degrees in Italian literature from Yale and Stanford. In addition to serving as the president of CAT, she is also a member of the board of the Center for Writers and Translators in Paris.

Patrizia Villani was born and lives in Milan, Italy, and teaches English at Università Cattolica. She writes in two languages. Poems in English appeared in journals *Agenda* (UK, 2002) and *Conjunctions* (website, USA, 2003); poems in Italian in *La Mosca di Milano* (online, 2004), *La Clessidra* (1/2005), *Poesia* (n. 195, 2005), *Poliscritture* (2009; 2010), *Il Monte Analogo* (2011) and a few anthologies, among them *Bona Vox – La poesia torna in scena* (Jaca Book, 2010) and *La memoria e l'attesa* (deComporre, 2013). Her published work includes the plaquette *Maestrale*, (Mme. Webb, 2008) and the book *Conversazioni necessarie* (Raffaelli Editore, 2011, foreword by Roberto Mussapi). The new collections *Sulle tracce dell'America* (a section of which appeared in the 2014 poetry almanac by Raffaelli Editore) and *Uncertain Geographies* are awaiting publication.

19061980R10117

Made in the USA
Middletown, DE
02 April 2015